Mending Your Money

How to Fix Your *Real* Financial Issues

RONNIE KINSEY

Copyright © 2019 Ronnie Kinsey

All rights reserved. No part of this book may be reproduced in any form or by any electronic or mechanical means, including information storage and retrieval systems, without permission in writing from the publisher, except by a reviewer who may quote brief passages.

Cover Art By David Payne at David Payne Design

Scripture quotations marked (ESV) are from the ESV® Bible (The Holy Bible, English Standard Version®), copyright © 2001 by Crossway, a publishing ministry of Good News Publishers. Used by permission. All rights reserved.

Scripture quotations marked (NLT) are taken from the Holy Bible, New Living Translation, copyright ©1996, 2004, 2015 by Tyndale House Foundation. Used by permission of Tyndale House Publishers, Inc., Carol Stream, Illinois 60188. All rights reserved.

ISBN: 9781797899466

DEDICATION

This book is dedicated to everyone who has ever struggled with money.

Who stayed up all night wondering what to do.
Who fought with their spouse day and night about money.
Who feared about their financial future.
Who thought there was no hope.

Know that there is hope, and that hope lies in you. You are going to get out of debt. You are going to start saving. And most of all, you are going to accomplish what you set out to do.

I believe in you and know you can do it.

Let the journey begin.

CONTENTS

	INTRODUCTION	1
1	THINGS AREN'T LOOKING SO GOOD	5
2	SPENDING WHAT YOU SHOULDN'T	23
3	YOU NEED A PLAN	47
4	WHY DEBT ISN'T JUST BAD, IT'S EVIL	73
5	FAITHFUL WITH LITTLE, FAITHFUL WITH MUCH	93
6	SAVING AND INVESTING	109
7	SOWING AND REAPING	125
8	THE POWER OF CONSISTENCY	137

ACKNOWLEDGMENTS

To my wife, Jen, and my children, Connor and Cailyn.

Thank you.

Your love means more to me than you'll ever know.

INTRODUCTION

So, there I was, sitting at a local coffee house staring at the floor while thinking about money. Not that I needed more or that I didn't have enough, but about how it's such a central part of our lives. Just the day before, I got a call from someone who was having money trouble, and their story really stuck with me. This person was around $25,000 deep in credit card debt. He and his wife were starting to get behind on their mortgage, and they were at risk of losing their home as well as one of their cars. During the conversation, he told me that he and his wife were living paycheck to paycheck (which is true for roughly half of all Americans) and falling behind fast. Yet, about halfway through our talk, he switched the topic. He began joyfully telling me about the amazing 7-day cruise his family had taken just a few weeks earlier. How on earth did his money trouble and the joy of an expensive cruise he took end up in the same conversation?

Thinking later about this story, I realized that this scenario wasn't just scary—it was sad. I was puzzled over how things had gotten to that point for not only this man's family, but also for countless Americans all over this country. This man and his wife weren't technically broke. They had great jobs and even had incomes that were well above average. But their pockets were completely empty. They were up to their eyeballs in debt, and they were at risk of losing their house and cars. As all these thoughts whirled around in my head, I was baffled about how things had gotten this way for so many people.

As I thought more about money in general, I also considered the power it has over us. I mean, think of its pervasiveness in the life of every person on the globe. Wherever you live, take a day to go out into your community and think about a few things you may not see at first. Think about the fact that every single adult human being you lay eyes on uses money. Every . . . single . . . one! Yet if we all use money, shouldn't we be pros at it? Well, clearly we're not. Actually, we're far from it!

And it gets worse. You are no doubt aware that around half of all marriages these days end in divorce. A quick peek at some surveys that asked what led up to a divorce reveals that the culprit is many times their finances. Go and chat with some married couples that you know. Ask them or anyone else you encounter what leads to arguments with their spouses, and money will nearly always come up. You see, whether we like it or not, our finances affect us in a way we may not want to fully admit. Money has a place in our lives that is much bigger and stronger than any human being may ever consider. Although if we take an honest look and give an honest answer, it's clear that we are failing in how we manage money as a society. If we could get our finances together, we could drastically change our lives.

So, look, before you even keep reading, let me explain a few things about what you're getting yourself into here. This book is not complicated—not in the least. You don't need to know crazy algorithms or to revisit your high school math classes to get your finances where they should be. The principles that get you from where you are to where you need to be are simple. This book covers plenty of practical steps; but once you get your mindset where it needs to be, you'll be moving farther and faster than you ever thought possible. With that said, you need to know that the principles are simple, but doing what is needed and continuing to do it is going to take work. No one is saying that having a complete turnaround in your finances is going to be easy, but it will definitely be worth it!

Chapter 1
THINGS AREN'T LOOKING SO GOOD

Money. We chase it, worry about it, and stress over it. But, if we really take a look at this money thing, we may be surprised how easy it is to get it right. I mean, it's just pieces of green paper we put in and take out of our wallet, right? Well, you and I know that there's way more to it than that. While writing this book, I wondered about the level of anxiety people reading it may be feeling about their financial situation. There are money issues all over the world, and they eat at the minds of so many people. And, of course, that's why we are here. That's why you and I are going to take this journey. While there are a lot of people who have abysmal financial situations, it doesn't have to stay that way. Things *can* be better, and they *will* be better.

As we take a journey together to work on our financial life, I think it's first important to consider what the problem actually is. You may want to open up the first chapter here and get right to work. And while we are definitely going to be getting to work soon, there's something we need to do first. We need to get to the bottom of our money issues. Yeah, that's right. We need to first understand what on earth has landed so many of us in financial trouble. When we can get a grasp on what got us here, we can take purposeful steps to make sure it never happens again. Once we do that, we can also tap into our minds and see why we do what we do—especially when it comes to money.

What Are the *Real* Issues?

You may have read the book's subtitle and wondered why I mentioned our *real* financial issues. So, let me tell you my take on it. As you may imagine, I routinely study and read books that have to do with finances. When I read these books, I notice that the word "millionaire" comes up all over the place. There are books galore on how to think like a millionaire and become a millionaire. Don't get it twisted—being a millionaire is great! Yet, as I talk to people all over America, I ask myself, "Is it millionaire status that everyone needs?" Is the fix for our financial woes that we all need to be millionaires so we can pay our bills? Or is it something much deeper than that?

Honestly, I see the American financial landscape

suffering from a much more critical issue. It's not that we lack millionaires and that if everyone was toting seven-digits in their bank account, all our problems would go away. No, it's much different than that. See, it's not a "lack" issue; rather, the issue is what we're doing with what we have. In certain parts of the world, there may be severe poverty. That type of issue is serious, and it's because of genuine lack. Yet, I just don't see that problem here in America. In America, I see people who are making more money than they ever have, and yet their financial situation is worse than ever. Of households that carry credit card debt, the average debt is around $16,000, just in credit cards alone. That is horrendous! We have to take note of epidemics like this and take immediate action to eliminate them.

When I sit down and have conversations with people, I see a disturbing trend of debt and financial ruin. What typically sends the biggest chill down my spine is not usually the conversation about money woes, but how the whole thing goes down. It's not uncommon for me to make an appointment with people who are having financial trouble, and they drive up in a shiny new car or brand-new pickup truck. They are miserable about their financial situation, sobbing about the position they're in, and all the while the idea of trading in their brand new $40,000 car sitting in the parking lot hasn't even crossed their mind. And when I make mention of it, they look at me like I just asked them to give up their first-born child. This is no isolated incident; it happens all the time. And please, if this is you, don't be offended or upset. I'm here to shake your conscience a bit and get you on the right track. Once I can get you to see what's going on, I can help you change your financial life for the better.

Hear me out on a few things. You might be shocked to know how many people I've encountered who have been in tears over their financial situation and then have proceeded to tell me about how great their $800 vacuum cleaner is? And how I *must* get one! It makes me absolutely want to pull my hair out! Again, don't take it the wrong way. I'm not making fun of you or demeaning you; what I am doing is begging you to consider a different way of thinking. This book is about how the issue plaguing America has nothing to do with the fact that we simply aren't millionaires. It's that we have the most messed up financial practices of any civilization that ever existed. And in the direction we're going, things are not likely to get any better. We need to return to the simple basics. We need to understand the mindsets behind why we're doing what we're doing. Then and only then can we get things where they need to be.

Progress Is Our Friend, Right?

There's a glaringly obvious thing happening. In case you haven't noticed, we live in a world of progress. I mean, think about it: We have phones so smart that they can order a pizza, scan a barcode, and look up any information we can possibly want to know in an instant! If that's not cool, I don't know what is. Yet, with all this progress, it seems we are going backward with our financial lives. We have technology that can wirelessly transmit a conversation, yet average Americans can't balance their income and spending.

Picture the financial situations of your five closest friends. How do they look? If you and your friends all sat down together and talked about where you were with your financial lives, how much debt would be discussed? On average, how much savings would you all have? And how much of the debt that you all have would be accumulated on credit cards? I say this because the reality is that if you're experiencing financial trouble, you need to know that you're not alone. I'm not saying it's good. I'm just saying that it's something that is happening to a lot of people, and we need to work to end it and not just get comfortable with it. And while most of America is in the same boat you're possibly in right now, you're about to jump ship.

The Pursuit of Stuff

As I've likely made clear in just a few pages, I'm usually not one to beat around the bush. So, I'm just going to go ahead and say it: Here in America, we love *stuff!* From cool cars, to lavish houses, to designer clothes—we love it all. Now don't get me wrong; I like nice stuff too. But I also live with the understanding that there's a price to pay for everything. And more times than we care to admit, we spend more than we should. When I'm out and about, one of the things that is so glaringly obvious is that people are all out chasing *stuff*. And, for the most part, they don't have the money to pay for it.

Our consumerism can be quite addicting. Let's face it, when you drive down the road, when you turn on the television, and when you surf the web, you are constantly bombarded with someone trying to sell you something. I'm okay with people selling stuff, but we have to learn that just because something looks good or seems useful, we don't need to buy it. Think about it: Have you ever wondered whether you can go just one day without someone trying to sell you something? Well, no, you can't.

I went to a shopping mall the other day and had one store in mind I wanted to go to. One . . . single . . . store. On my way to the place I was going, I had to go by all the little kiosks that vendors were operating. As I walked by, I felt like I was approached by someone trying to get my attention to buy their product every 10 seconds. It was maddening. If you've been to a mall, you have to know what I'm talking about. It would seem that consumerism has taken the reigns of our attention and focus. And if we're not careful, we'll get pulled in.

Look, these vendors that were talking to me had some cool stuff. Their colognes smelled good. The phone cases they had were cool, and the people who were offering back massages almost got me to bite. Don't worry, I resisted. But see, this *stuff* is what is causing our money to leave our pockets a little too quickly. And once we know this, we can be on the defensive. Some of this stuff looks good, some of it feels good, and some of it tastes good. And trust me, the people trying to sell it to you are well aware of the fact that it's something you might want.

Take a stroll onto a new car lot and you'll see. There's a salesperson who comes out to talk to you and they fully know the price of the vehicles. And while salesman are many times great people, they are by no means trying to help you retire well. They aren't going to remind you that you need to be saving for your children's college fund. And they definitely aren't going to try to help you accumulate a certain amount in your savings. They're out there trying to tell you how good you are going to look in this brand new

$55,000 pickup truck you're eyeballing. Now, I'm not saying that it should be the salesperson's priority to keep your financial future in mind, but it definitely needs to be yours!

Not only does this type of thinking need to go for cars, but it also needs to go for everything! Take the Internet. When you are online, you are in the middle of marketing central. Ads for things you have looked at or purchased are constantly popping up. Have you considered how much time and money these companies have spent trying to figure out how to make a person buy their products? They have it down to a science! Unless you are actively trying to avoid them, your subconscious mind can get eaten up by your desire for this stuff. And I am not making some type of diatribe on why you don't need to buy things or why shopping is bad. The thing I want to get into your mind is this: What's messing us up is our desire to have more things.

It's the Person, Not the Possessions
We, as a society, have been duped into thinking we need things that we most certainly do not. Day after day we buy certain products, thinking that we need them or thinking that they make us better as a person. Frankly, many see their possessions as what makes them worthwhile

individuals. Thinking that having a certain possession makes you better off is nothing short of vanity—actually, *it's a bit more like insanity.* The simple truth is that what makes you a more worthwhile human being is who you are as a person. It's not what car you're driving, not what type of sunglasses you wear, not what brand of jeans you have on. If you can realize that it's your character that makes you who you are and that Gucci® jeans and Levi's® jeans both perform the same function, you will achieve a sense of freedom that you may have never known was possible.

Adopting this mindset is a big step in moving forward. If you can grasp this early on, the process of getting your finances together will be way easier. Getting this type of thinking in your mind early will help you in your financial life more than you can imagine. It's so important that it's the first thing I wanted to share with you as we take this journey. While you may be wondering why I am discussing this so early in this book, it's because I know that once we can get this simple foundation under our belt, the rest of our time together will flourish.

Culture

I have to admit I love social media. It's a great way to connect with people, and it has great benefits. While some accuse it of making us less social (which I'm not technically disagreeing with), I think the reality is that it causes us to live in an artificial world. I mean, let's be honest; how often do you see a selfie of a husband and wife saying, "Look at us! We're arguing over money again!"? It's likely not going to happen. Social media is, at best, a highlight reel—a fanciful life lived out to see how many likes you can get. But there's something going on you may not notice. See, you open it up and begin to scroll by your friends' posts. You keep scrolling and then, at some point, you run across a celebrity. Maybe the person is a household name, or maybe just someone highly admired in your social circle. You scroll through your social media or maybe flip through your favorite magazine, and you notice that the celebrities are wearing top brand-name clothes. Maybe they're even riding around in luxury cars and have enough diamonds around their neck that it makes me wonder how they are able to keep their head up.

The issue is this: As soon as you lay your eyes on a famous person, whether you know it or not, you are being persuaded to believe that what is shown is the standard. That is, the standard of success for anyone trying to be *somebody*. And trust me, everyone wants to be somebody. Once we have seen where the bar is, we have to meet it. So, we go out and get a new car, $200 sunglasses, $150 jeans, and $250 shoes. (A lot of times these items may be priced even higher;

I'm being conservative.) We take pictures of ourselves with our new clothes, cars, and accessories and scream, "Look at me!" And you know what? You get affirmation for it. This is now a standard that people chase, and it seems like the world is applauding. The applause you get causes you to ignore the consequences and to tread forward, oblivious to the dangers ahead.

I'm not suggesting that you not follow certain people on social media or not read certain magazines. If you like those things, then certainly go ahead and enjoy them. What I am begging you not to do is this: Look at a person who brings in $30 million a year and try to keep up with that person on your $45,000 a year salary. What may actually surprise a lot of people is that it's very possible that the person you look up to who makes that $30 million a year is blowing every single dime of that money. Aside from blowing every single dime by buying tons of luxury items, that person may reach a day when he or she doesn't make that much money anymore. What if that person's $30 million turns into $3 million a year? Or worse yet, what if it turns into $0? Know that these things happen.

You can do a quick search for professional athletes who went from broke to millionaire overnight and later back to broke again. And because of debt, they may be even worse off than broke. This is no isolated incident. It's happens time and time again. There are many people who come into money and then spend it on *stuff* quicker than you can say, "How exactly did you spend $10,000 at the mall in one day?" We laugh and make jokes, but these things happen. While these big spenders may be great people, their financial practices are anything but great. And they are practices you need to be aware of and that you never need to repeat. Have all the friends you want, but make a decision to be a person who is healthy in your financial habits.

Mindset

The whole problem with the majority of money issues stems from mindset. You can call it what you want, but behind society's financial troubles is a mindset problem. You may be shaking your head and blaming the problem on a manipulation of numbers or cash flow. But hear me out. I know people who buy brand new cars at a time they have absolutely no business owning a car that costs that much money. When I talk with them about their finances, I routinely tell them to sell their car and get one that costs less than half that amount. When I say that, most of the time, they look at me like I just grew antlers or have only one eye.

The reason I get this look is because people attach their worth to their stuff. And when I tell people to sell their car or downsize to a smaller house, they feel that I just told them to trade in who they are. It's proof they identify who they are with what they possess. Some may never want to admit it, but many people feel that if they live in a $400,000 house, they are better than those who live in a $200,000 house. They believe that if they drive a BMW, they are better than those who drive a Honda. *It's this type of mindset that causes person after person I encounter to end up broke.* These people have an income—usually, one that's not too bad. They just spend it like they have an all-access pass to Warren Buffett's bank account. Once we can get this mindset right, we're moving in the right direction towards where we need to be.

Bit by Bit

All of this doesn't happen overnight. It's gradual. Suppose, for example, you decided to eat fast food for every meal for the rest of your life, you likely wouldn't die the first day. Yet over the course of many years, you might run into some health issues. It's the same with finances. A purchase here, a purchase there, and the problem snowballs faster and faster with each swipe of your card. It happens over time, usually not in a day.

When you started paying with credit for things you didn't have the money for, the world didn't come to an end. You got your credit card bill, made the minimum payment for a year straight, and kept charging. And guess what? Your roof didn't collapse on you. Well, for now at least. But one day you took the time to look at the new balance on one of the five cards you had done that with, and you started to get a little sick to your stomach. You realized that there is no way to pay off all the debt you have accrued. You realized that the lender is about to foreclose on your home, your car could be repossessed, and the cost of the clothes and nice dinners you charged is building up interest that makes it impossible to pay off your debt. And at the rate you are going, things are about to implode. This situation happens over time, and it happens to a lot of people. I didn't pick overspending as my first topic by chance. This type of spending and thinking is so prevalent, it's scary. But as soon as you diagnose it, you can be on your way to curing it and being where you need to be.

Kick It Out!

At this point, if what I'm saying is resonating with you, you need to hold your head high and not despair. Beating yourself up isn't going to help anyone, so don't go there. But there is one thing that does need to happen. All of the spending has to stop—immediately! Have you ever heard the story of the 30-year-old who lived at home with his parents and didn't have a job? His parents walked in one day and kicked him out of the house. Sounds pretty rough, huh? Well, I need you to have the same thought process as those parents. Whatever it is that has caused you to think that you need this *stuff,* I need you to kick it out of your head.

Think about that same 30-year-old who ate all his parent's food, didn't contribute nor work toward anything, and got kicked out because he was a freeloader. Well, you need to do the same with your freeloading thoughts. Yes, there are thoughts in your head that are freeloading. How can that be? They sit in your head and tell you all these things that you need, and they eat up your resources while contributing nothing. Kick them out of your head and move on with your life toward financial happiness.

Take a Stance

When I was a kid, I used to play football. What's interesting is that I was actually an offensive lineman. Now, you may shake your head and wonder why that is so interesting. If you have never met me, I am just shy of 6 foot 3 inches tall. I currently weigh about 175 pounds, and I love distance running. So, yeah, you're likely not picturing me as an offensive lineman. But when I was younger, I played that position and was frankly awful at it. But I remember one thing from that time: I used to take a 3-point stance, and when the quarterback said "hut," I would not only block, but attempt to drive the defensive lineman out of the way.

If I knew the running back was going to be coming by my left or right side, I would do what I could to drive that defensive lineman the other way. What I remember is that if I just stood there, the other team would run me over, tackle the running back, and I would feel like a moron. But if I kept my feet going and thought about driving the other person backward, it usually happened. Think of that as you work toward bettering your finances. You can't just stand there. You have to drive the opponent (i.e., debt, bad spending, compulsive shopping) backward and take territory for yourself. That territory represents being debt-free, with savings in the bank, and a retirement plan.

If you always keep this in mind, you can take quick action to reorient yourself in the right direction. Take a stance today that you are sick of overspending, sick of the debt, and sick of looking at a checking account with $17 in it. Take a stand that you are sick of the five credit card bills that have thousands of dollars owed on each of them. Take a stance that you are done with the fear of collection agencies—done dreading a letter from the bank saying it wants the car back. Take a stance that all this irresponsibility stops today. *Then*, start to take action to end it and to turn things around for the better. The quarterback has started the play, and it's time to make things happen.

This Isn't a Joke

As you can probably tell, I am passionate about finances. And I want you to be too! Look, I have seen financial issues drive people into misery and despair. I have heard stories of people who committed suicide over their financial situations. These stories are true, and they happen more frequently than you may think. So, yes, I get fired up when the topic of finances comes up. When I do, there are always a few people that say to me, "Ronnie, what on earth is your problem, man? You are getting too intense about bad spending. It's just some clothes and sunglasses. You need to chill!" Well, I don't need to chill, and we actually need more people that get upset about these things. Personal finance issues in America are at full-on epidemic levels.

Here We Go

Okay, we're almost off and rolling on getting your finances where they need to be. And frankly, where your financial mindset needs to be. At the outset, I want to let you know that you have laid some groundwork for getting control of where you stand in your financial life, and now you are going to start going piece by piece through what you need to do to get a good grip on your situation.

One of the first things I want you to do is get a financial journal. And that financial journal can be anything. It's really just a place where you write down financial-related notes. It doesn't have to be something fancy. It can be a 99¢ spiral notebook you get at a discount store. You can use a computer, tablet, or even a phone to record your notes, if that's how you want to do it. You just need a means of writing things down and taking note of what you learn, what you need to apply to your life, and what you need to take action on.

If you can start to write down what needs to change and what you are going to do about it, it will revolutionize your life. Writing down goals and action steps on paper or anywhere else is magical. The process takes a thought and gives it life. It becomes something tangible and real, rather than something you are just talking or thinking about. I will refer to your financial journal throughout the book, so have it handy while reading. Again, it's just somewhere to put your thoughts, ideas, and takeaways. Get ready, because it's time to get started!

Chapter 2
SPENDING WHAT YOU SHOULDN'T

Every single conversation about money *can* be a struggle. *But it doesn't have to be!* It is, though, going to be work. Some people think there's a magic wand you have to wave to fix your finances. Others think you have to travel and discover the solution from a guru on the other side of the planet. I'm here to tell you that there are no secrets. As a matter of fact, there's a possibility that I'm going to tell you things you may have heard before. If I tell you something multiple times, take it as a clue that the advice is important, and you need to apply it immediately.

As you may suspect, a lot of times when I talk to people, they ask me questions about money. The conversation and topic may vary, but routinely it may go like this:

"Ronnie, if you could give me just one single piece of

advice on how to be better with money, what advice would that be?"

"Well, I'm glad you asked," I say. "The most important thing is, *Stop spending money you don't have!*"

"Wait . . . What? . . . That's it?"

"Yep, that's it!"

If we, as a society, could just chew on this statement for some time, it could drastically change the landscape of American personal finance. If we could put it into practice, we could change the world. And trust me, if this statement sounds like one of the simplest pieces of advice on the planet, it's because it is. But is it the one that we mess up the most? Absolutely!

Look, when it comes to spending every red cent that enters our pocket, Americans reign supreme. When it comes to spending more than we make, we hold the gold medal. At this day in time, it's practically a badge of honor to be in debt. We're used to the idea of high-class credit—with our platinum credit cards and lines of credit. Living off credit has become a norm in our society.

Bear With Me Here

Is "Stop spending money you don't have" really the top advice I have for you? Actually, yes, it's first on a long list of many things. But before you shrug it off as it seems impossible, take a moment to consider a few things. At first glance, to not spend money you don't have seems to be a no-brainer. If I have $5 cash in my hand and walk into a store, I can spend only $5. Yet, spending is so much more complex than that now. Most people have moved well beyond a cash-only system, and this has allowed some pretty interesting things to happen when it comes to spending.

As you already know, you can walk into nearly any department store in America, and someone will give you a nice little plastic card that will allow you get whatever you want. You can walk out of the store without any money actually leaving your hand—at least, for the moment. And this trend goes well beyond just department stores. You may get credit card offers in the mail all the time. They come in beautiful packages telling you that you are "pre-approved," and this makes the world seem bright and happy. Well, while the packaging may be bright and happy, the reality of what can happen with credit cards is far from it. We'll come back to credit cards and how they work a little bit later.

The point is that American spending has morphed to where just because you get to zero doesn't mean that you're done for. You can go well past the $0 mark and just keep on trucking into the negatives. It's this type of spending and thinking that has absolutely devastated family after family that I talk to. The issue is that this is short-term thinking, and it completely abandons any chance for long-term financial health. As you progress in getting better with your spending, you will learn to look at things in relation to how they contribute to your long-term financial health. Those who think only about short-term pleasure lose sight of the effect their spending can have. Unfortunately, this short-term thinking can often lead to making detrimental financial mistakes, which carry heavy penalties.

To stop spending money you don't have is simple and powerful. What is astounding is that while it's powerful, it eludes a vast majority of Americans. Why? I would say that it comes down to the fact that we have created an instant-gratification culture. People want it, and they want it now. This type of culture rewards only the "now" mindset, which, again, is an abandonment of sound thinking. If you want to get your finances to where they need to be, you have to spend money that you actually have and also spend less money than you make. Again, these principles are easy, but hard to swallow for many people that are working to better their finances. Don't fall into this instant-gratification trap!

Basics

As you can see, what we are doing here is not some advanced calculation to determine how fast the earth rotates. As we start off, we are going to work on the most basic things of personal finance. Why are we starting with things that are this simple? Because if you want to be great at something, you have to master the basics! It's the basics that make people great in every area of life.

Don't believe me? Take one of the world's greatest athletic coaches, John Wooden, for example. He won 10 NCAA basketball championships in a 12-year period. Seven of them were in a row! Something about Coach Wooden's success you need to know is that he was all about the basics. As a matter of fact, when new players arrived on his team, one of the first things he would do is give them a lesson on how to properly put on their socks and shoes. I am not kidding! It's something that we laugh about because it seems so absurd, but one of the greatest coaches of our time did this. And he's not alone. Winning coaches are absolute sticklers for basics.

Your finances are going to be the same way. Throughout this book, I am going to hammer away at what seems like the simplest things in the world. And while they are, they are going to be what propels you to financial freedom. Now let's get cracking!

Where Are You Now?

Our first hurdle is to look at how much you currently make and how much you currently spend. Right now, you may be getting cold sweats because you know that this reality may not be a pretty sight. Taking a hard look at your bank statements could very well be like looking at chewing gum on the bottom of your shoe. This step, though, is essential! Stay calm and assure yourself that you can take this first step toward getting your finances together.

Take time to gather all your bank statements for the past 6 months. You may need to open your online banking account, pull out your credit card bills, or go and sort through all your unopened mail to see what you have. Whatever your means, *I want you to collect what you need to be able to track your income and spending over the last 6 months.*

Income

First, we will go over income. As you look over the statements, note your income per month and then add up how much you have made over the last 6 months. You will want to get out your financial journal and grab a calculator as you get started. Once you have those things in front of you, let the adding begin. In all, you could be adding income from the one job you have. It could be your main job and the one part-time you have. It could be all your jobs and your IRS tax return you got back recently. Whatever it is, add up every bit of income that you have made over the past 6 months. You will want to calculate a monthly total and a 6-month total; you will need both later. Have these numbers in your financial journal, because we will write them in a table in the following pages.

Understanding Income

As you probably expect, when I talk to people about their financial situation, the conversation often gets into income and expenses. Though income and expenses might seem like basic information, I *rarely* talk to someone who knows exactly how much he or she makes and spends each month. As a matter of fact, when I meet someone who *does* know how much he or she makes and spends, I'm usually taken aback. People are always telling me, "Well, I guess I make about . . ." or "I don't know how much I spend, I just pay what I can on the credit card bill and hope it's more than the minimum." These replies make me cringe. It's not too difficult to see why so many people cross the line in their spending. This is also a reminder of why I am having you calculate these to the penny while we are early on in our time together.

While figuring out how much you make may seem painfully simple, you need to understand the nuances of it so you can plan how you're going to manage your spending. For the most part, people know what their salary is by the hour or day, but they don't really have a grasp of what their monthly income is after taxes. I need you to know the amount you bring in each month down to the penny. It's in your financial journal now; just be sure you are aware of it. Remember, if you don't know how much you make, how will you ever know how to budget?

Now you may wonder why I regularly mention a "per month" time frame. There are a few reasons. A lot of expenses, like mortgages, rent, car payments, and utility bills, usually come on a monthly basis. So, we use monthly amounts for our calculations. Monthly totals also are helpful for budgeting, which we will get to soon. For budgeting, everything will be in monthly percentages. If you don't know the income you have, the percentages of spending that income will be useless to you.

Fluctuating Income

Some of you live off a paycheck that doesn't budge. By this I mean that you have a certain amount that you make each week, every other week, or each month, for example. But some of you have an income that moves around. You may make a certain amount one month, and then the next month, it could be half or double that. The variation makes it difficult, but there's no need to fret.

If your income is stable, and you know how much you get, you will track monthly income with monthly expenses. If your income fluctuates, you have a couple options. First, you could use an average. For instance, if your monthly income ranges between $3,000 and $3,500, you can choose the average of $3,250. Alternately, you can play it safe and use the lower number. I personally would recommend using the lower number, because it's just another tool to propel you toward living below your means. If you set your monthly spending and you use the income marker of $3,000 a month, then when you have a month that you make $3,500, that's a time when you bank an extra $500 in savings. You may be tempted to spend it, but if you can keep your hands off of it, you'll be quickly surprised how fast you can accumulate some savings.

If your income fluctuates a lot, you may have another issue on your hands. But it's nothing that can't be managed. I have friends who work on commission, and their income can vary widely. If you're someone who has varying income, here's what I suggest. Calculate your averages over a long period of time. Instead of using 1 month, maybe you could use a 2-month or 3-month average. Honestly, you may even want to see what your 6-month or yearly total income is and find an average from there. What this does is help you calculate an income that gives you one number to work off of so that you can set your spending habits in a safe and manageable way. Once you have your income set, then you can use it as the basis for making quality purchases.

Whatever income point you pick, be conservative and remember that your goal is to stop spending more than you make. I say this so you are sure the line you use as your income isn't inflated. It's better for it to be calculated too low than too high.

Understanding Spending

Now that you have your monthly income worked out, it's time to get rolling on those expenditures—or simply put, what you spend your money on. This is where your blood pressure may go up, but don't fall out on me; better times are on their way! Go back over your bank statements and/or receipts and calculate the number that you spent in total each month. You can expect it to fluctuate, so you'll be looking at the ebb and flow of your spending habits. Having your monthly expenditures in front of you will give you a real and accurate picture of how much money is leaving your pocket each month.

You have 6-months of numbers for monthly income, so now you need a 6-months of numbers for monthly spending. Be sure to write them in your financial journal. While this task may seem arduous, remember that very few people take the time to do this—but those who do almost always come out on top. Why? Because once you identify your spending habits, your mind will work subconsciously to remedy the problem areas. Know that you mind can work as a supercomputer. Once you identify the things that are messing up your financial life, you can then begin to be more aware of them in your day to day life. This will make it easier to eliminate spending temptations when you are faced with them. You can't eliminate a problem that you aren't aware of, so take this time to know what you spend and know where your problem areas are. It may seem difficult at first, but believe me, you will see the results.

Use Table 2.1 to help you make some calculations. Fill in the spaces for each of the 6 months of income and expenditures you have calculated. You have already written these monthly totals in your financial journal. All you have to do with the first two columns is transfer the numbers you have written in your journal. What you will also need to do now is use a calculator to complete the last column of the table: For each row, subtract the monthly expenditures total from the income total. In front of each number in the last column, enter a "+" for a positive number or a "–" for a negative number. For clarity, let's go over the elements of the table so it makes sense what we are doing here. When you have saved money during a certain month and stayed under budget there will be a "+" beside the number in the final column. When you have gone over budget and lost money during that particular month, there will be a "–" beside the number in the final column.

Table 2.1. Income and Expenditure Totals

Month	Total Income $	Total Expenditures $	Difference (+/–)
1			
2			
3			
4			
5			
6			
Totals			

As you calculate the numbers, reality should set in pretty quickly. Again, be sure to calculate *all* expenses. Just because you swiped a purchase on a credit card and can pay later doesn't mean it's a "later expense." One of the goals we will be setting as you get your finances together is to see everything as cash. If you don't have the cash for it, you don't get it. The overall goal is to know for a fact how much money left your wallet and your bank account, as well as how much you spent using your credit card. Include all your expenses—whether via cash, debit card, credit card, check, or any other means. If you spent it, you have to calculate it!

Once you get the last 6 months of income and spending written down, take a cold hard look at it. While it may not be pretty, it's something that can help you as you understand the reality of your financial situation. Table 2.2 shows an example of what your completed chart may look like. We'll go over some numbers in this example so you can see the impact this information can have. Again, a "+" denotes you stayed under budget and saved that amount, and a "−" denotes you went over budget and lost that amount of money.

When you look at an example like this, you can see where things can quickly go. Some may say, "Hey, the guy here only went over half the time; that's not too bad." But this person spent $1,500 over what he made in only 6 months. That's $3,000 a year if that type of spending continues. In a decade, this person will be $30,000 behind. And here's the worst part of it: If this guy spent more than he made, it means he likely spent on credit. And any spending on credit means there's interest to pay back as well. So, this $3,000 of overage each year is well on its way up.

Table 2.2. Example of Completed Table

Month	Total Income $	Total Expenditures $	Difference (+/−)
1	$3,500	$4,157	− $657
2	$3,500	$3,406	+ $94
3	$3,500	$3,455	+ $45
4	$3,500	$4,193	− $693
5	$3,500	$3,798	− $298
6	$3,500	$3,491	+ $9
Totals	$21,000	$22,500	−$1,500

Clearly, the situation in this example is not what any of us wants. If you see something like the example here in your own notes, your first goal is to spend less than your monthly income total *every single month*. Another good thing to do at this point could be to go into your financial journal and see where you are for the year. What that can do is give you a macro and micro idea of where you stand on income and spending. This may be difficult because you will need more material to see what you have earned and spent. Although, I can guarantee the reward will be well worth it as you grow closer to seeing all the spending that has been done.

Don't beat yourself up if you are quickly realizing that your income is less than your spending. While this is common and one of the biggest financial mistakes I see people make, it's one that can easily be corrected.

Before moving on too far in the book, you may want to go back again to see what your spending looked like for the past year or maybe even 2 years. Go back as far as you need to so that you're sure you have a good grasp of your income to spending differences. *This is one of the most basic and critical understandings you'll need as you progress.* There are a few reasons why stepping back at this point is so important. One is that if you don't get this right now, your spending pattern will follow you for the rest of your life. If you make $60,000 a year and overspend on that, you are more likely than you may think to overspend later when you might make $100,000.

I see it all the time. Someone's income goes up, and what does the typical family do? Upgrade the houses, cars, toys, and everything else you can imagine. For the average person, when income goes up, every other type of spending goes up as well. But this doesn't have to be what you do. And don't necessarily think that more money is the answer to your financial situation. Getting your spending where it needs to be should be the first step. Then you can start thinking about adding wealth.

It's time to grab your financial journal and write down five things that you overspend on. Take time to think about what these things are and how you can work to overcome your need for them. Maybe you can think about how you need your money more than you need those items. Either way, write them down and begin to think about how you can eliminate or reduce these expenses in your life as you work to get your spending where it needs to be.

Where Are Your Priorities?
At this point, things may get tricky for you. I know, as if they haven't been difficult enough already. You have looked at your income and your expenditures and are thinking, "Now what?" While we will get into budgeting in the next chapter, we need to do some preliminary thinking and consider some questions. Once we do that, we can get into planning what to do with your money. The big question I want you to consider for now is, "Where are my priorities?"

As we move along, you'll see that a lot of this book is about determining what you want. If you love spending more than you make, love being in debt, and could care less about bettering your financial life, you likely wouldn't be reading this. Perhaps you just really love reading or just love me and figured you would give this book a shot. While I'm honored if you do love me, I still need you to get going on your finances. I am going to assume that if you're still reading this book, it's because you do want to get better with your finances. This is likely in addition to wanting to get out of a financial hole. If this is the case, you need to ask yourself again, "Where are my priorities?"

Place to Place

Priorities keep us straight; they keep us on track with what we want and what we need to do to get there. If you want to drive from Atlanta to Los Angeles, for example, you hopefully have a few priorities. The first is a means of transportation. If you don't have that, you will be walking, and that may not be exactly what you had in mind for that type of distance. Let's say on this journey that you have a car and start driving. You quickly see that having gas in the car is going to be a priority. If that's not a priority, your car is sitting dead on the side of the road, or certainly will be soon. Maybe you have all the car issues in order, have gas, and are driving toward Los Angeles. But you don't take time to consider that it takes roughly 32 hours of driving to get there. Do you drive without sleeping? Do you divide it up into two long stretches? Do you make it in three? These decisions all have to do with your priorities for this particular trip, and your financial situation is no different.

As you look at your financial life, you need to realize

what is important to you. What are your deal breakers? What are your must-haves? Maybe you want to change jobs, or maybe you want to stay in the one you're in forever. If given the choice, some people would rather have a job that provides 6 weeks of vacation time with a $30,000 a year salary. Some would rather have only 2 weeks of vacation time with a $45,000 salary. It depends on personal priorities, and now is the time to think about yours. Once you know what is important, you can reorient yourself in that direction so you can achieve that desired result. Just like driving from Atlanta to Los Angeles, you need to know *your* direction.

What this means is that you need to know where you need to go. Do you need to stop buying clothes each week? Do you need to stop going to steakhouses for dinner every other night? Do you have to have a certain type of car? If you see you are headed in a direction you don't want, make the decision now to turn around and go in a different direction. Make the decision to set priorities along the way so that your financial health will overrule your desire to spend on things you want rather than need.

Challenge Everything

When I was younger, I used to be in law enforcement. While that profession has its positives and negatives, one thing that always intrigued me was the criminal justice system. As you may have suspected, I spent way too many hours of my life in a courtroom. Yet, the thing that always seemed so interesting to me is that anything and everything is challenged in a courtroom.

I have heard lawyers make all types of arguments in various court cases. One day, it could be that I arrive in court for a DUI case, and the lawyer goes off on a tangent about how the blood test can't be trusted. Or about how it was late at night when the arrest happened, and his client was tired. About how the officer was likely tired. How a car's steering wheel is naturally made to cause someone to swerve. How a certain brand of tennis shoe can cause someone to be unable to walk a line. I think you get the picture. What's interesting is that some or all of the things the lawyers bring up may or may not be true. Yet, either way, the lawyers work them into their arguments to make a case for their clients. The case could be either for or against the accused. They argue whatever they can to get the case to go in the direction they want.

What I want you to grasp is that you need to do the same thing with your finances. No, I don't want you to put them on trial for DUI—although some people have spending habits that may make me question their sobriety. What I want you to do now is to question every penny that leaves your pocket. Should I be buying this? Is this a need or a want? Questions like this can make huge differences in your life.

When you look at your spending habits, ask, "Is this really necessary?" And get in the habit of questioning expenses on a large scale. When we get to actual planning, we'll look at a more detailed way of thinking. But for now, look at what you spend and ask whether each item is necessary. Moreover, ask what is necessary for you to live given your current situation. Many times, once people get ahold of this truth, they realize it's way cheaper to live their lives than they ever imagined. They also realize they don't need millions of dollars to be happy.

To the Max!

So many people I know make a decent yearly wage and spend every dime of it. What's interesting is that most who make, for example, $100,000, could live off of $80,000 without really losing too much quality of life. Those who make $80,000 could live off of $60,000. You get the picture. There is this idea out there that you *have* to spend what you make. But it's just not true. Think of it this way: For a person to go from spending $100,000 a year to $80,000 a year may seem like a tremendous drop—but it's not.

Ask yourself a few questions. Is there that big a difference between a $100 pair of jeans and an $80 pair? Is there that big of a difference between a $100 dinner for the family and an $80 dinner for the same family? Is there that big of a difference between a $20,000 car and a $16,000 car? There isn't actually that much of a swing in all of these choices.

Yet these simple 20% reductions could produce a savings of $20,000 a year for someone who normally spent $100,000. Rather than spending all or more of what a family makes, a family could make small adjustments. And if they save that $20,000 a year rather than spend right up to their income line, they could have $100,000 saved in just 5 years. That's amazing! In 20 years, they could have accumulated $400,000 from just reducing things a small percentage, which they likely won't even notice. But guess what? They will for sure notice the $400,000 they have saved.

It's not complicated. I said that from the get-go, and I will continue to say it. These principles are easy. You just have to put them into practice. You just have to get turned in the right direction and keep going that way.

So, let's put what you've learned into practice. *Literally, sit down with your financial journal and begin to write down things that are not priorities in your spending.* Think of things that you can stop spending your money on right now. This can be all sorts of stuff and likely may be a long list. When you begin to put these items down on paper, you'll be able to see the toll they're likely taking on your finances.

You may even want to write down how much each item is costing you, and then add that up over a month, 6 months, and a year. Once you see the price tag on something for a year, the truth really begins to sting. If you spend $5 on a pack of cigarettes every day, you are spending $1,825 a year on them. And that's if you only smoke one pack a day. That means that a person who brings home $40,000 a year would spend nearly 5% of that income on something he or she can do without. So not only do you have a good excuse to quit because cigarettes aren't good for you, but they are eating your money as well. Take the time to see what these non-priority expenses are and eliminate them fast!

How Much Is Enough?

Let me help bring this home for you so you understand what it means to live beneath your means. Ask yourself, "How much is enough?" No, really, how much income is enough? Is it $40,000 a year? $100,000 a year? $1,000,000 a year? Who really knows? You do, that's who!

I see people time and time again live perfectly fine at a certain income level. And sure enough, when they get a raise, their spending goes through the roof. Do they stay at the same level of spending and invest or save the remainder? Of course not! They go out and spend the new income like it's burning a hole in their pocket. It happens every single day in America and all over the world. What's sad is that it's not healthy and it has to stop.

I see people who live on a $70,000 a year income and are perfectly happy. Yet when their income goes to over $100,000 a year, their spending goes way, way up. They end up miserable because they have created financial disasters with their spending. I beg you, don't do this!

You have to know what to challenge. Ask yourself, "Do I really need more stuff?" Continue to ask, "What is more important? More safety and security in my financial life, or more things that are going to wear out and depreciate in value?" These are huge questions to consider as you go forward in your financial life. Challenge your spending to be sure it's what you need to be happy. Challenge your thinking about the goods you need. Challenge what car you feel you need to drive. Challenge how big of a house you need to live in. Challenge it all. It's worth the effort—trust me! Don't accept the poor habits of your past to continue to manifest. Take action today and take ownership that you are going to get things right!

Chapter 3
YOU NEED A PLAN

By this point, you should have a really good idea of what your spending versus income differences looks like. If you don't, take some time to go back and nail that down before progressing. You should also have a grasp of the idea that you need to live below your means and that the sooner you cut unneeded expenditures, the better off you'll be. Now that you're here, you're ready for the monumental task of making a plan for your finances. Yes, it is monumental, and yes it seems daunting. But it's really simple if you just take the time to do it.

As a matter of fact, just a few minutes of calculating and planning can save you thousands of dollars and remove boundless amounts of stress from your life. Yet, like so many other simple processes in this book, many people don't take the time to do them. So, push forward and don't fall back into the needless spending trap again. Listen, you need to know how much you make, to have decided how much you want to spend, and to have a plan for that spending. It's that easy! Let's dive in and take a look at a few ways that you can plan out your finances.

What Is a Plan?

I know, you probably read that and said to yourself, "Does this guy honestly think I don't know what a plan is?" I know you do, but I want you to think of plans in a new way. Not just for finances, but in every area of your life. There are some people that have plans and some that don't. Some people have plans for everything, and some people don't have plans for anything. What you need to accomplish right now is to create a plan for how you spend your money. If you don't do this critical piece of planning, you're missing a lot of the needed process for getting your finances together.

Planning in Action

I live near Atlanta—a massive city with one of the biggest airports in the world. From where I live, I'm close enough to see planes in the air constantly. Now let's say you and I take a trip together to the Atlanta International Airport.

When we get there, we get a backstage pass to not only fly for free, but also to accompany a few pilots as they go through their day. As we start to watch the pilots, we quickly observe that they have a plan for everything they do. They have a plan for what time they need to get to the airport, and they have a plan for which gate they need to arrive at. They also have one for when they should leave the gate and where they are going. But it doesn't stop there! They have a plan for what route they are taking to our destination, they use a charted course throughout the flight, and they know from start to end each step they should take at each moment.

Now, let's flip the script. Let's say you and I land in another city and hop on another plane. We'll be hanging out with a different set of pilots now. We get up to the cockpit of the plane, and two guys are up there wearing jeans and T-shirts and sipping coffee. When we step on board, they ask us, "Hey, you don't happen to know how to fly this thing, do you?" Terrified yet? Wait, it gets even worse. These guys were recruited to be the pilots from the local restaurant in the airport. Not only that, but they have no idea where they are going and for sure don't have any points plotted to get us to the next city. As a matter of fact, they don't even know how to start the engines on the plane.

Which one of these two planes do you want to be on? It's a no-brainer. You want to be on the first plane I described. Why? Because there was planning and preparation. The pilots took time to know how to fly, they knew where they were going, and they knew how to get there. They also expended a lot of effort to get it right. Those pilots regularly do whatever is in their power to get things done correctly. And you know what? Plane after plane leaves that airport and gets to where it's supposed to go.

But here's the cool part: Your financial life is just like that! If you take the time to learn what you are doing, know where you want to go, and follow the simple plotted course outlined in this book, you will be well on your way to where you want to go with your finances. If you don't do those things, however, you will be the other two guys who have no idea what they are doing or where they are going. The choice is easy, and the choice is yours.

Still not sure? Well, consider this. One thing my kids love doing is going downtown. They think skyscrapers are the coolest things ever. As we approach the city, they are in awe of how massive the buildings are. My wife and I usually grumble because of all the traffic—but that's a different story. Did these structures just happen along by chance? Maybe some construction workers got bored and threw some metal and concrete together during their lunch break. Well, of course, that didn't happen. Those skyscrapers are a product of some of the world's greatest architects. Everything was carefully planned, down to every nail, beam, and wall. And, guess what? After years of careful planning and hard work, every major city in the world has some beautiful buildings.

We all know that it takes lots of planning to build a skyscraper. Yet, in every major city all over the world, people think that financial success can just happen. I am here to tell you that it can't. Just like the pilots and just like the architects, you have to make a plan and see it through. Make the plan and stick to the plan; it's that simple.

Budgeting

You may be shaking your head a bit now and thinking, "No one is going to tell me how to spend my money!" Well, actually someone is. And that someone is you. Budgeting is the backbone of getting to financial health. Trying to grow to financial maturity without budgeting is like bodybuilding without lifting weights. Unheard of! If you are going to grow to financial maturity, you need to budget. I can promise it's not going to be so bad. It's time to roll up your sleeves and plot a course to your destination.

The idea of budgeting is simple. You have already

figured out how much you make and now you are going to figure out how much to spend. What is daunting here is that you may be wondering where to start. Rest easy, friend; help is here.

As you begin to budget, you have to face some realities. There are some expenses you can control and others you can't. Here's some guidance for these two realities.

Some expenses aren't going away.
While you may be able to give up some expenses quickly—like an overpriced drive-through breakfast each morning—other expenses aren't going to be as easy to erase. Take your home, for instance. If you own a home and your house payment is $1,500 a month, that expense is going to stick, at least for a while. It's not one you can cut tomorrow. Sure, you could sell your house, but then you would have to pay closing and real estate fees, as well as find another place to live. You don't need to make any drastic changes like that on day one. But know that for some people I counsel, I have recommended that they sell their house and get one that is drastically cheaper. You may be in that situation now. If you are, take time to work through a budget and make a firm plan for what is needed. Don't just stick a "for sale" sign in the yard without having a plan. For now,

you may just need to settle on a good budget and start living within your means.

Cars are another expense that may or may not be controllable. Many of us need a car to get to and from work, especially where public transportation is not always available. If you have cars, take the time to evaluate whether they are a need or a want. I personally buy cars that are used and drive them until they are 10–12 years old. I do this because it allows me to pay cash instead of having a car payment. And the car does what I want it to do: Get me from point A to point B. I have challenged my belief on what car I need—not the car I *want,* but the car I *need.* If I had the best sports car made, I would be sacrificing my financial health so I could go fast. If you want nice fancy cars, hold off until you are financially able to afford them without breaking your budget. If you are trying to get your finances in order, now is not the time for bling. It's time to get healthy.

Some expenses can be cut quickly.

As you consider the budget you are about to make, ask what you can cut. Not only what you can cut, but what can you cut immediately! Do you need a $5 coffee on the way to work every day? Of course, you don't. If you calculate what that costs 5 days a week for 4 weeks, that's $100 a month. You could make coffee at home for less than $1, or actually much less than $1. When you take a close look, you may be surprised how much you are spending on food. Eating out at restaurants quickly raises a food budget. You can make the same food at home that you would eat at a restaurant for a fraction of the cost. If you are looking to save, look no further than a grocery store, and let that restaurant go. While restaurant owners certainly want to make you happy, their primary goal is to make money. As business people, they need to charge more for the food so they can pay the staff, cover the cost of the space they occupy, and make a living. Go to the grocery store and make the food yourself. Keep that extra cash in your own pocket.

Cutting back on entertainment is another way to immediately remove items from your expenses. Entertainment is such a sacred cow in America. When I talk to people about cutting entertainment, they always give me the "but I deserve it" speech. This area is easily one of the top things that cause people to stumble in spending. Take the time right now to Google the price of two people going out to a movie. Add up how much it is for them to go to the movie, share a large popcorn, and each have a soda. Where I live, this would be well over $40; it may be even more where you live. You can watch a movie at home with popcorn and soda for a fraction of that cost. Of course, it's not the same experience. But wanting these types of experiences on a regular basis is usually an issue when budgeting.

Entertainment regularly comes up among the biggest issues when I counsel people about their financial situation. If you find yourself wanting these experiences, take time to look for deals or bargains. Aside from hunting for deals, save even more by eating your own food before you go out at a fraction of the cost of a restaurant. It's the *mindset* I want you to work on here. The movies aren't bad, their popcorn is fantastic, and the soda is refreshing. It's the price point of these outings that you have to be aware of. The movie theatre isn't evil—I love movies too. But please adopt the mindset that gets you into the practice of making these experiences fewer in number. They also need to be at price points that make them more in line with your budget. Trust me, you'll thank me in the long run.

Vacations are the final topic I want to discuss among the quick-cut items. Don't take this the wrong way, but it almost makes me fall over when I hear some vacation stories. Not where and what, but how much was spent. It's not uncommon for someone with tens of thousands of dollars of debt, no savings, and living paycheck to paycheck to go on a vacation that would strain even the best of checkbooks. There are fabulous places you can go for a getaway that won't melt your wallet like some of the spending I've witnessed. Bora Bora is a great place, but if you are not financially secure, you only need to see it in pictures.

So, look, I'll go easy on you here. I'm not exactly telling you not to go on a vacation this year, but you may want to consider that option if you need it to stay afloat. What I am telling you is that you need to be mindful of how quickly expenses add up on a vacation. I also want to communicate that you don't need to be extravagant to have fun. If you want to spend a few fun days at the beach or somewhere else, there are plenty of price-friendly options available. Instead of staying at the nicest hotel on the block, take your time and do some research online to find more economical lodging. You don't have to stay at a luxury resort to enjoy yourself. Search online for deals and consider the price first, and then the amenities.

On top of the costs of travel and lodging, the cost of meals during a vacation adds up quickly. Just know that you don't have to go big on every meal, as I see a lot of people doing. A vacation is about getting some food and spending time with family or friends. My wife and I go to a grocery store and make our own food on vacation. It's our time together we cherish, not the restaurant we're at. I would advise you to take the same stance. Time with family and friends is free; expensive hotels and restaurants are not. Keep the main thing the main thing when going on a vacation.

Grab your financial journal and start jotting down notes on how you can start cutting back on some of these expenses. It may seem difficult at first, but once you start writing notes, you will begin to come up with fresh ideas for conquering some of your expenses. For me, when I see something on paper, it ignites my thinking and helps me uncover solutions for fixing the problem. Jot down some notes and tackle those difficult money thieves.

Spending Percentages

As we talk budgets, the time always comes when we need to look at our spending and set percentages for each category. Setting these percentage allocations puts bumpers on to keep us where we need to be. If we know that housing, for instance, is 20–35% of our spending and we make $100,000, our yearly spending on our house needs to be $20,000 to $35,000. And with that said, we would like to keep it as close to $20,000 as possible.

Let me preface the budgeting portion here with a

statement: There are lots of different ways to set your budget allocations. If you get on the Internet and look at budget percentages and budget worksheets, there are so many that it may make you want to immediately close the browser window and give up. There are just too many. I am here to eliminate a bit of confusion—to help give you some clarity. Again, while there are a lot of variations, I have put together an easy model that can hopefully help you as you start to track your spending. I keep it simple so that it makes sense and so that I can easily explain it to you, and also so that you can easily keep track of what you are spending. This budget may differ slightly from other ones you have seen, but I want you to go over it and consider the benefits you can gain from its use.

    Housing 20–35%
    Giving 10–15%
    Food 5–15%
    Healthcare 5–10%
    Savings 10–15%
    Utilities 5–10%
    Transportation 8–13%
    Insurance 10–20%
    Personal 3–8%
    Fun 2–5%

Let me first explain something that is usually not explained in personal finance books. If you do the math, you can see that all the minimum percentages add up to 78, and all the maximum percentages add up to 146. There are ranges because you won't always be able to be exact in your expenditures. You will have to stay within range and realize that things will fluctuate. Also, these ranges allow you to adjust your spending across the categories. Know from the beginning that you can't always use the largest number because it's going to send you over budget. You have to see where you are in each category and work as best you can to get each one down. If you are well below in one area, you are going to have to figure out where to reallocate that money. I always recommend taking that extra money and putting it towards the savings category. If you can make the cut in each area and grow the savings portion, you are well on your way to winning.

Now we can look at each of these categories in turn and see what spending goes in each one. Keep in mind that if you can go under the lower percentage in any category, that is amazing. When you go low in any one area, it allows you more wiggle room in another place. But if you go over, it is a red flag and you need to evaluate that area immediately and figure out how to trim it down.

Housing 20–35%

Housing is a big expense and obviously you need it. If you have nowhere to live, things are quickly going south. This category includes not just your mortgage payment or rent, but also things directly related to your home— furniture and décor, repairs and maintenance, homeowner's insurance, and taxes. So, don't just look at your rent or mortgage payment; there's more to it than just that. Your biweekly landscaping and anyone cleaning your house for you can also go here. A lot of people max out this category and buy a house that is at their 35% range. Then they go out and get brand new furniture and décor, and totally blow the budget. Don't be one of those people. Please, if you can, keep this as close to 20%, if possible. If you are able to go below that, more power to you!

Giving 10–15%

You are probably scratching your head on this one if it's new to you, but I couldn't be more honest here. If you want to get your finances together, giving is a must, not an option. More times than you can imagine, people who have wealth are people who give. We will talk more about the topic of giving later. But it's important to note that true wealth and long-term financial health always include some type of a giving element in it. There's no way around it!

Food 5–15%

This one is set at 5–15%. If you really want to get things together, you're going to want to just go ahead and pencil it in at 5%. This category includes food at the grocery store and restaurants. You can always eat out less, lay off the lobster, and choose cheaper options. A big pot of spaghetti and sandwiches can quickly be your friend here. Usually bringing this number down involves fewer restaurants and buying food that is at better prices. There's a lot of ways to save here so be creative. Trust me, it's beyond doable and you will come to enjoy cooking at home if you just take the time to do it.

Healthcare 5–10%

We all know that sooner or later a doctor's visit is on the agenda. It's not something we want to say, but it's the truth. You will use this area for those doctors visits as well as any medicine that is required for your proactive and reactive healthcare. This category includes things like doctor/dentist bills, braces, glasses, contact lenses, as well as prescriptions and over-the-counter drugs. Also, any surgeries, co-payments, and health-related expenses (other than insurance) will go here.

Savings 10–15%

You need to start saving your money. If you aren't doing this, start today. If you go above the set percentage mark, this is the one area that I'm good with you doing that. This will be the category that will later be used for retirement, financial investments, your kid's college tuition, and any other savings initiatives you want to have. Be sure not to cut this one too close, as it's the area from which wealth will begin to emerge. If there is any area you want to "go-big" on, this is it. This is the one category where you get paid, so remember that its one that you don't want to mess up. Keep in mind, you can't go wrong with keeping more money in your pocket, rather than it going out towards things that you don't need.

Utilities 5–10%

One way to save here is to not waste electricity. I say this because it's one of the ones that is easy to do. Turn off the light switch when you leave a room and keep the house a little warmer in the summer, a little cooler in the winter. The savings can be huge. This category includes electricity, water, gas, phones, phone plans, trash, cable, and Internet. Most things in this category can be trimmed back, so be sure to keep an eye on the expenditures at all times. This is the category where some painful truths come in. One is that just because Apple® comes out with a new phone, it doesn't mean you have to have it. I know, that can be difficult for a lot of us, but you'll thank yourself down the road if you hold out.

Transportation 8–13%

Getting from place A to place B is a must. A brand-new car is not. This area includes not only cars, but everything related to them. This category includes all car payments, gas, oil changes, repairs, tires, also tag and license fees. Keep an eye on this category as it can get big quickly if you don't pay attention. A nice car looks good on the lot and also in your driveway. The issue is that most of the time, the payment that comes along with it doesn't look so good.

Insurance 10–20%

Insurance is a must. This category includes things like car and life insurance, and health, dental, and vision insurance. These all add up but can save you money in the long run rather than paying out of pocket. Get good rates and be sure to have insurance in the areas you need it. Having health insurance may not be the cheapest thing in the world, but paying out of pocket for a major surgery can cause a pretty severe blow on your bank account or debt balance. Again, home and renters insurance goes under your housing portion of the budget.

Personal 3–8%

You kids need clothes, you need clothes, and your hair needs cutting once in a while. This is the category for those items. There are great ways to save here. You can save on a lot of things if you avoid impulse buying and always shop smart. If you're behind financially, you can get a Coach® purse later. For now, get your finances where they need to be. Things you would put in this category include clothes, toiletries, hair care, child support, school tuition and supplies, as well as gifts.

Fun 2–5%

Yes, a category for you and only you. Vacations, movies, entertainment, whatever it is you want can go here. The savvier you can be on your spending here, the more things you can get, so be careful what you choose and don't blow it on one purchase. This is one that can get away from you so be careful with it.

What About Investing?

Work toward getting financially healthy. Once you master the basics of spending and saving, then you can work toward investing. Remember that savings category? Once you get some savings under your belt, you can begin investing after that. For now, concentrate on saving until your finances are where they need to be. We will discuss investing in a later chapter in the book.

What About Debt?
I am glad you asked! Your ability to pay off the debt you owe is directly tied to lowering every single spending category. If you want to pay off more debt, but also go to the movies, guess which one needs to be the priority. If you want new shoes, but want to pay off debt, guess which one needs to happen first. It's all again about priorities. Paying off debt needs to be high on the list! Just so you know, we will go over paying off debt in depth in a later chapter.

Budgeting on Paper
I am always going to encourage you to keep a written budget. It can be electronic (including apps) or on paper, but make sure you always have it in some form of writing. I say this because having a budget on paper or on a device, where you record where your money should go, helps keep it from floating away. Of course, it doesn't float away; you spend it. But you get the picture. If you have a plan for every single cent of your income, then it's all accounted

for, and it will keep you from wasting and impulse spending.

Now go back to Table 2.1 where you plotted 6 months of spending and income. Identify your *worst* month of spending and use it to fill in Table 3.1 to create a visual of where you stand. Write your income for that month here (_____) so you can reference it as you complete the table. Take the time to categorize the spending of that "worst month" you picked out. Once all your expenses for that month are categorized, you can add up the totals and put those amounts in the Total $ for Category column. Then, using your monthly income that you wrote on the above line, calculate what percentage of that month's income is in each category.

Table 3.1. Budget Allocations

Category	Total $ for Category	% of That Month's Income
Housing		
Giving		
Food		
Healthcare		
Savings		
Utilities		
Transportation		
Insurance		
Personal		
Fun		

To make it easy, you can Google your math questions

(e.g., "200 is what percentage of 3,000?"), or you can use your phone's calculator. Here's an example. If you spend $200 in a category and made $3,000 that month, it would be 200 divided by 3,000, and you get 0.066. You then just move the decimal point two places to the right and you get your answer, which is 6.6. So, if your monthly income is $3,000 and you spent $200 in one category, that category is 6.6% of that month's income.

That's all the math you need for this. Repeat the process for each category and put it all into the table. Once you see where your spending percentages lie, you can go back and see whether they fit into the ranges we discussed. If anything is too high, write down in your financial journal ways you can cut back on spending in that area, and begin taking action on that today. Hopefully, completing this table will help you give a glimpse as to where you are doing well and where you are doing poorly.

Tools for the Journey

There are loads of free financial tools, budgeting apps, and financial learning programs available. If you get online right now and do an Internet search for any of these topics, there are so many that it can be dizzying. Don't be too overwhelmed by all of them; just know that they are there to help you. Why on earth am I telling you all of this? Because after you read this book, your journey isn't over. You need to be continuously learning and getting better at financial practices for the duration of your life. As a continuous learner, you can improve your financial practices and the way you handle your money. The minute you stop learning, you go backward.

After you get done reading today, take time to look up different financial tools online and see which one looks best for you. There is a plethora of good ones that are free, so you usually don't need to spend anything. A budgeting app is something I highly recommend and it's also something that is generally user-friendly. Take your time and find one you think will work well for you and the way you operate. When looking for one, don't pay too much if you actually end up buying one. Make sure it's easy, and more than anything else, be sure you use it. Looking at reviews from others can help you in picking one out. Typically reading what they say in these types of reviews can help you get a glimpse of whether you want to use the product or not.

Budgets Are Just Financial Diets

You may be thinking to yourself, "A diet? What? Not for me!" Don't freak out! Budgets and diets are very similar. They're both about breaking old habits and developing new ones. Diets come in many different forms. Some promise that you can lose 20 pounds in just 7 days. Others claim that you don't even need to change your diet; you can just take a pill or have a powdered drink and then just sit back and watch the pounds melt off. If you are anything like me, you are likely a bit skeptical about those claims. Why? Because that small voice in the back of your mind is telling you that it's not going to be that easy. And a financial diet isn't going to be that easy either.

Think about it, when you start a diet, things get tough very quickly. C'mon, we've all been there. You pick a diet to try, decide on a start day, and get off and running by eating a salad for lunch. Then 2 hours later, you start to panic because you are hungry again, and you are wondering whether you can keep going. Notice what I said here. You are "wondering" whether you can keep going. And that's the thing: It's in your head! You are sensing a change from the high-calorie garbage you may normally eat, and you want to go back to your former ways.

Like a diet, this same thing could happen with your new spending plan. If you are used to going to the mall every Saturday and charging hundreds of dollars on a credit card to buy clothes, guess what is going to happen when you don't? That first Saturday is going to arrive, and your mind is going to be wondering why you are not at the mall. You may sense that something is wrong, because what you're doing is out of the norm. Be aware from the get-go that it's perfectly okay not to be out needlessly spending money. Your mind may be in a panic, but tell yourself there is absolutely nothing wrong. You just have to keep going in the right direction and not give in to temptations to go back to old habits and things you know better than to do.

Persistence

How many times do you think people have started a diet? Similarly, how many times do you think people have started an exercise program? Well, the answer to both questions is likely a really big number. But what do you think those numbers would be if we changed the questions a bit? What if we wanted to know how many people have stuck with a diet or exercise program for a year straight? I can guarantee you that the number would be drastically lower. Why? Because it's easy to start things, but much harder to keep going with them. Although, there is one thing I can guarantee you: The people who are experiencing success not only started, but also kept going. It's the keeping going part that people get tripped up on. We start our diets, we start our exercise programs, we start our budgeting plans, but then we all too many times stop following them, and that's when we run into trouble.

A lot of getting your finances in order, like getting your health in order, is about persistence. This goes for most things in life, but it applies in big ways to your financial life. Doing something a few times may get you nowhere, always be sure to keep at it when it come to good habits.

You Know What to Do

Another thing that makes budgeting and diets similar is that the choices are obvious—well, technically. Think about it. You can go up to any person and ask what it takes to be healthier. You will hear about the need to limit fast food, to eat fewer calories, and to eliminate junk food. The person may also go on about the need to work out a minimum of 30 minutes a day, three to four times a week. Most people actually know exactly what they need to be doing in order to be healthier. Why? Because it's simple, and people know it! Most people know that eating fast food every single day isn't good for them, but they continue to do it. Most know exercising is good for them, but they never exercise. They continue these practices because, in the moment, it's better to eat the triple cheeseburger. In the moment, it's easier to lie in bed and sleep longer than it is get up and exercise for 30 minutes. And therein lies the key: The difference between thinking in the moment and thinking long-term. When you think long-term, it begins to change things. The same applies to finances.

In the moment, eating in a really fancy restaurant feels

better than going to the grocery store for food. In the moment, it feels way better to go and buy a brand-new car rather than to drive one with a few years on it. But in the long run, if we make these kinds of momentary decisions day after day, they begin to add up and can endanger our financial health. And this, my friends, is where things get bad. If you overspend just a little each day, over the course of months and years, it adds up to huge amounts of debt; and debt is likely not what you want if you're reading this book.

A Budgeting Lifestyle

We've gone over budgeting plans and how the model needs to work. What I need you to do is to stick to the plan! The key to a diet is sticking to it, and the key to making a budget work is the same thing. You can make this work, but you simply cannot give up. You may have to toy with the percentages and work on some things as you get your spending under control in certain areas. But once you get the hang of being within budget each month, it gets easier and easier as time goes on. This is a lifestyle you have to adopt, not just a one-time thing. Be patient, be persistent, and the results will come! No matter what happens, remember that giving up is not an option.

Chapter 4
WHY DEBT ISN'T JUST BAD, IT'S EVIL!

If I could crawl out of this book and into your life, I would do it to help you truly understand debt. I would literally get down on my hands and knees and beg and plead with you to listen to me. Why on earth would I do that? Why would I go to such an extreme? I'm glad you asked! The reason is that I have seen debt absolutely demolish people's lives. And I use the term *demolish* because that is what it can do to people. As I write this, there are millions of Americans spending themselves into a hole. And not a small one—it's one that is well over their heads, and the possibility of climbing out is bleak. Getting into debt is done way quicker and easier than getting out, and we need to do everything in our power to avoid it.

Every day, Americans are swiping a little plastic card or signing a dotted line to purchase things they do not have the money for. Watching this happen is frightening, yet so many people in our culture are perfectly comfortable with it. Please, if you are reading this and feel comfortable with debt, let me not only help you get your finances together, but also help you realize the monster that debt can be.

The Reality of Debt

Consider Bob. Bob just graduated from college and wants to do some big things. He's not really sure how to do them, but he begins the journey of life and seems to enjoy all the boundless opportunities before him. One of the first things he realizes is that he needs a car to get around. He goes to the car lot, where he finds many shiny new cars. He walks over to one and sees the price tag is a whopping $35,000. He starts to walk away but is greeted by a car salesman who begins to talk about the car and how great it looks. Bob agrees the car looks great but says he doesn't have $35,000. The salesman quickly replies that this is no problem at all and that he has a deal where Bob can get a car today for no money down if he qualifies. Bob is astounded that such a thing is possible. The salesman runs Bob's information and finds out he's qualified.

Bob is ecstatic yet is still puzzled. He wonders how much he will pay, and the salesman tells him he can get the car for a mere $693 a month. Bob scratches his head but believes he actually can spend that much each month. So, he signs the papers and drives the car home. What Bob is never told is that his brand-new car loses roughly 10% of its value the very instant it's driven off the lot. He also doesn't understand the 7% interest rate he just got nailed with on his new car. What all this means is that his car was priced at $35,000 but is immediately worth only $31,500 when it leaves the lot. What he also doesn't know is that after interest payments are added, once he pays for the car over 60 months, he will have paid $41,583 for that car that was worth $31,500 when he drove off with it on day one. When you look at the numbers, the car doesn't seem so much like a winner, does it?

But this is just the start of the bad parts of Bob's story. When he leaves the car dealership, he realizes that his new apartment needs some furniture. He goes to the furniture store in his new car and starts pricing some. Once again, he initially has sticker shock. But when the salesman comes over to him, he is assured that he can afford the payments. He has picked out a living room suite that costs $5,000 but knows he doesn't have that kind of money. "No problem at all," the salesman tells him. You can get it with no money down and have it delivered to your home in just a few days. He is told that it will cost only $132 a month. Bob again is ecstatic. He sees that he is getting the hang of this buying thing. What Bob doesn't really think about is that he has to pay that $132 a month at 12% interest for 48 long months. Also, the already high-priced furniture that is listed at $5,000 is going to cost him $6,320 by the time it's paid off. If it depreciates by the same 10% as the car as soon as it shows up at his house, he will pay $6,320 for furniture that was worth $4,500 after he sat on it the first time. Sounds awful, doesn't it? Hang onto your seat; it gets worse.

Bob gets home and is on top of the world. He opens his mailbox and inside is a credit card application. He has no idea how credit cards really work, so he calls his old college roommate. His roommate tells him that he can take the card to stores, swipe the card in the checkout machines, get stuff right away, and then pay later. Bob feels that he has had tremendous success already paying on credit, so he applies. And you guessed it! In just a short time, his credit card appears in the mail. The credit card is such a deal; but it unfortunately has a 17.5% APR (annual percentage rate) on his purchases. He then goes out in his new car, after sitting on his new couch, and starts to buy stuff like a madman. He only has a $10,000 credit limit but charges the card to the max in the first month.

Reality Sets In

Bob then runs into his good friend Mary. He tells her about his new card and the spending he has done in the first month. Mary is a smart saver and is troubled by what her friend has done in such a short time. Mary starts telling her friend that he has done something that he will regret. He says to her that he doesn't understand what her problem is and that he can pay later. Mary asks what his interest rate is and how much he can afford to pay per month. He gets out the paperwork and tells her the interest rate is 17.5% on the card. As Mary cringes, she reluctantly asks how much he can pay each month to pay back the money. He tells her he can pay only $200 cash a month to get it paid off. The one good thing is that the bank that issued him this card put his minimum payment at a flat 2% of his balance, which at that moment came out to be $200. So, he could indeed meet the payment for the minimum balance. Bob is still a bit nervous, so he uses his phone's calculator and sees that $10,000 divided by $200 is 50 so he can have it paid off in a little more than 4 years. Mary shakes her head and lets him know that it likely won't quite work that way.

Indeed. It doesn't work that way at all! Compounding interest is an insane concept—sometimes with consequences you can only imagine. With a $10,000 balance, a 17.5% interest rate, and only $200 to pay each month, it will take Bob 91 months to pay off his credit card debt, and he will have incurred more than $8,000 in interest payments. Again, with paying $200 a month, it will take him 7+ years to pay off the $10,000 debt, and he will have paid almost double by the time it's all over. His final bill at the end of the nearly 8 years would be $18,044.

The Numbers Don't Lie
Bob, after the end of this conversation, is not doing so well. While this may sound like a pretty extreme case, it's actually not too far from reality for a lot of people. I regularly talk to people with tens of thousands of dollars in credit card debt. They have no plan to get out of debt, and they are sometimes moved to tears to even think about the position they are in. Granted, if Bob could advance his $200 payment to $300 a month, it would make his payoff time only 46 months instead of 91. It would also make his total interest paid $3,795 instead of $8,044. But the point of this whole story is this: Debt and interest will eat you alive. The only way not to get into this situation is to—you guessed it—NOT to get into this situation. I have had a credit card since I was in college. And every single month except for maybe a few, I have paid off the card in full. I had heard these types of horror stories when I was

younger and vowed never to make these types of mistakes, and I beg you to avoid them as well.

You can read this story about Bob and do a few things. You could shrug it off, you could weep at how it isn't that far off from reality for many people (possibly including you), or you could consider it a wake-up call and take action. This is not a joke. Sometimes the specifics may be different, but overall, credit cards and credit card debt are absolutely demolishing American families. The sad part is that people are doing it to themselves.

The Scarier Truth

What may be surprising is that there is an even scarier version of Bob's story. It's a story that may land close to home because it could spell out how you ended up in credit card debt yourself. Not only are there people like Bob who don't understand what is going on, but there is an even larger portion of the population that is fully aware of what is going on and just keeps on digging deeper into debt. Some know good and well they have to pay later, they know good and well that interest is about to eat them alive, but they just keep on swiping that little card to appease that small inner voice that says, "I want it *now*!"

If this is you, don't lose heart and don't take offense at what I just said. That is not going to do us any good here.

What I want is for the light bulb in your head to go off and for you to have a moment of realization where you get mad. Yeah, that's right, I want you to get mad! I want you to get downright ticked off about what happened with your finances and to take note as to where it has landed you. The reason I want you to get angry is because that is what's going to bring about change. It's apathy that can get you into these positions, and it's anything but that which is going to get you out. Though I want you to get mad, I don't want you throwing things or getting upset at anyone. I want you upset at what bad financial habits have done to you and to get to a place where you'll do whatever it takes to get your finances right.

What If It's Too Late?
There is a possibility that you are reading this, and you are already in the predicament that Bob put himself in. If you are, I need you to listen to me. It's going to be okay. I do not want you to beat yourself up or think less of yourself. What I do want you to do is *stop spending money you don't have!* Start today! Don't wait until tomorrow or the next day. Do it *now!*

    The first thing you have to do is make a plan for how to get out. This is where the budget you created comes in handy. When you are trying to get out of debt, every penny counts. You could see that in Bob's case, the difference $100 a month extra toward paying off his debt resulted in 45 fewer months of payments. It saved him roughly half of the total interest he would have had to pay. While thinking about the amount of interest is heart-stopping, I mention it to let you know that paying off debt is an immediate concern that you need to take care of quickly. Start now, be smart, and be patient. The one thing to consider is that no matter what financial trouble you have gotten yourself into, there is always a way out. You just have to be patient and trust the process. And above all else, keep going and never give up!

Paying Off Debt

As you approach paying off your debt, here's the first thing I want you to do. *Grab that financial journal and begin making notes of all the debt that you have*. You may need to go and get your statements, but it's imperative you know the following information about *all* of the debt you have. Once you get an idea of the debt you have, check out Table 4.1. There you can write the person or entity you owe in the first column, the total amount you owe in the second column, the number of payments left, what the interest rate is, and what the minimum monthly payment is.

Table 4.1. Debt

Person Owed	Total Owed	# Payments Left	Interest Rate	Minimum Payment

Once you have that information written out, you may be wondering how in the heck you are supposed to approach this. Know I'm here to help. There are typically two ways of going about paying off debt. One is paying off the debt with the highest interest rate first, and the other is paying off the smallest debt first. I am a bigger fan of one of these methods, though the other also works well. Let me give you a quick illustration so you can see why I suggest you should try one way over the other.

I played golf in college. I wasn't exactly Arnold Palmer (I was far from it, actually), but I did well enough to compete at a collegiate level. No matter what tournament I was playing in, I had a routine that I followed. Here's how it started. The first thing I did before each tournament was to walk over to the putting green, drop three golf balls on the ground and putt them all in from about 6 inches away. You're probably going, "Ronnie, 6 inches? A 2-year-old can make that!" And you are absolutely correct. I purposely did this because the first thing I wanted my mind to embrace was me making putts. I pulled those three golf balls out of the hole and repeated the process multiple times before moving on to practice putting from farther distances. Again, I did this to train my mind. I wanted to make sure that the first thing I did on the golf course was to make 10 or more putts. I did this rather than starting off from 10 feet and making only a few. My first task was to make 10 putts, and I did it every single time. My subconscious mind was already used to me sinking putts first thing.

The reason I shared that story about golf is that I want you to apply that mindset to paying off your debt. I want you to train your mind toward success. So, take another look at these tactics for paying off debt. Remember, one is to tackle the higher interest rate first, and the other is to start with the lowest amount owed. *I favor starting with the one that has the lowest amount owed.* Momentum is a powerful thing, and if you can get going in the right direction, there's no stopping you! Look at your list of debts again—the list of people to whom you owe money. Imagine if in a few short weeks, or months, that list grew shorter. That would make you feel good, right? Of course, it would! That's what I want you to do. Just like the short putts I used to practice making, I want you to tackle that debt list by eliminating lines. And guess what? If you can start doing that, you will gain some momentum.

If you pay $300 a month toward one creditor and the minimum toward the others, once that $300 debt is gone, you can add $300 a month to the next one you tackle. Let's say that you owe $100 a month on the second one you are tackling, and that was what you had been paying as the minimum. Well now with that $300 added, you can pay $400 a month. And once that debt is paid off, you will have $400 a month to allocate toward the next one you want to knock out. And this just keeps going until you're done with debt completely. This is a proven way of getting out of debt, and I implore you to approach it head-on as you knock out debt and move toward financial freedom.

As I close this discussion about paying off debt, let me impart some knowledge. A lot of people I talk to would prefer to knock out the debt with the highest interest rate first. It's no secret that there are two schools of thought, and many people favor one over the other. I told you why I like paying off the smallest balance first and why that is what I feel is best. If you absolutely feel you need to pay off the highest interest rate first, go for it. I'm okay with you using a different tactic, as long as you stop unnecessary spending and start paying off debt. Both approaches are tried-and-true ways to get the job done. Just choose a route and go that way. Get after your debt and don't look back!

If you are wondering where this money will come from, note the "savings" category in your budget from Chapter 3. Your goals will be to begin saving money, accumulate a small amount of savings, and then pay off debt. It looks like this:

1. Start saving as described in the budget from Chapter 3.
2. Accumulate $500 in savings.
3. Begin to pay off debt.

It's that easy!

Once you're out of debt, you can then begin to save for retirement and invest for your kids college and other future endeavors. Again, all of this will at first come from your savings category, so the money you can save in other areas has a direct impact on how quickly you can get rid of the debt that you owe.

The second thing I denote here is to accumulate $500 in savings. This is because while I want you to pay off debt and start saving for retirement, I also want you to have some money in the bank. This is to help you in case you need any extra cash for any emergency that may come up. Of course, you have budgeted, and there is room for these types of things in your budget allocations. Nonetheless, it is good to have some money on hand in case of an emergency. And, as you may know, looking at your savings account and seeing a number that can barely get you a value meal at a fast food restaurant is not what anyone wants. I use the $500 mark because it's a good round number that can cover most simple issues that arise.

Remembering What Got You There

While the preceding plan is destined to work if you can stick with it, there is one thing that will cause it to fail. And that is continuing to spend more than you have. What got you into debt was spending money you didn't possess. And guess what can keep you from getting out of debt? Incurring more debt as you go along. If you are in credit card debt and you still have those credit cards, I want you to stop spending on them, *today!* Some will advise you to bury them, some will suggest you freeze them, and frankly, there are many ways to approach this. Well, let me give you my plan. I want you to destroy them! No need to go back and read that again because you read it right: *destroy them!* You can cut them up, blow them up, magically teleport them to another galaxy, or whatever you want. But they need to go away. If you want, you can even go out in your back yard and have a little funeral service before you destroy them. Whatever method you choose, make sure they go away. You are on a new path now, and if credit cards got you into this predicament, they aren't going to get you out of it. Make them disappear and get out of debt. You won't regret it.

The Cash-Only Option

Another way to keep from going further into debt and to help you cut spending is to use a cash-only system for certain expenses. After reading that last paragraph, you may have destroyed your credit cards, so you might already be looking for an alternative. I've got you covered! A cash-only system is good for getting certain things under control. Here's how it works. If you want to avoid unnecessary spending, go back to the budget table—Table 3.1—and find the areas where you typically overspend. Then make a decision to pay those expenses with cash only, and not to use any type of card, check, or electronic funds transfer for them. You put the cash in an envelope and label it with that budget category, so you know what it's for. When it comes time to spend, you know where to go and how much you have to spend in that category.

Now imagine how this would go on a typical day. Let's start with your entertainment budget that you would have in the "fun" category, for example. Say you tend to overspend on that. What you would do to is take that month's budget for entertainment and put the cash in an envelope. When it comes time to go to the movies on the first day of the month, you reach in there and can see how much you have. By the end of the month, you can see you have some left, or at some point you reach in to use it and it's gone. No matter what, you can spend only what's in the envelope. This practice will help you get a better handle on your spending. And I don't know about you, but when I use cash, I feel it! If I swipe my card and spend $100, that is one thing; but when I hand someone a $100 bill, I feel like my pinky finger went with it! There's just a certain sting to it that you feel. That sting is good and can help you in your endeavors to stay out of debt.

The Good Old Joneses

The expression "Keeping up with the Joneses" has been around for a long time and depicts the idea of keeping up with your neighbors in appearances, social standing, and basically, making sure you have all the cool stuff that other people do. The whole race that we put ourselves in when attempting to do this drives me bonkers. I've watched it for most of my life, and it's absolutely insane. All over America, people buy houses they can't afford just to "look" like they are well off. Maybe someone goes out and finances a high-end car or always wears name-brand clothing so they "look" like they are doing extremely well financially, when they aren't even close to living in financial health. If this is you, I beg you to stop it now. This type of lifestyle only gets worse as time goes on. Even as I write this, I just had a conversation with someone who financed a brand-new car, spent more than $1,000 on a single day of family entertainment, and at this moment has a single-digit bank account balance. And, unfortunately, if you get down to the bottom of it, you'll see that all this spending was done in the name of keeping up a certain social standing. It breaks my heart to see and hear these stories over and over. Please know that I am here to help you stop this type of spending. And, more importantly, please know that what you own doesn't equate to who you are.

There's something you need to know about "keeping up with the Joneses." The "Joneses," so to speak, aren't even people you want to "keep up" with. Once you see what they are doing, you see they are actually moving backward financially. The debt cycle is mean and will chew you up and spit you out. If you buy stuff that you don't need just to keep up with people who you likely don't care about in the first place, what on earth is your goal anyway? If your neighbor has cool stuff, yet is up to his eyeballs in debt, do you really want to be like him? The average person is neck deep in debt and trying to be like that person will land you in the same place.

Time to Go!

The moment has arrived when you may get sweaty palms. If you owe $30,000 on a car in your driveway and you can't make the payments, or they are putting you further into a hole, it's time to get a different car! You don't need a luxury car; you just need something to get you to where you need to go. You simply do not need most of the things that are holding you back. I have watched people I know and love drive a car on which they owe in excess of $25,000; and, all the while, they live paycheck to paycheck. When they needed a lawnmower for their half-acre yard, they bought a top-of-the-line zero-turn riding mower instead of a cheaper push mower. It's this type of spending that has to stop.

Not everything we buy needs to be the very best available. Look at what you are buying and what its purpose is. Ask, "Will this get the job done?" There's absolutely no need for a guy who has only a half-acre yard to buy a $3,000 lawn mower. He could have gotten a good one to do the job for 10% of that price. But he let the "Keeping up with the Joneses" attitude creep in, and that can be devastating. It has to stop, and it has to stop now!

Grab your financial journal and jot down some items

you have purchased that you know were "Keeping up with the Joneses" items. Your list might have just a few items or maybe a lot of items. If you are in deep debt or facing serious financial trouble, consider how you could downgrade some of those items or even get rid of them altogether. Remember, every little thing counts, so take your time in figuring out what to do while bringing your expenses down.

Reflecting

I want you to do something for me now. I want you to sit there and think about all the stuff that got you into debt. No, really. *Take the time to come up with all the ways and all the purchases that caused you to get into debt and write them in your financial journal.* The reason I want you to do this is that once you can identify what got you there, you can make sure it doesn't happen again. This exercise isn't a sick way of torturing yourself; it's a way to identify a problem. In business, if things go south, you want to figure out what went wrong. Well, in your finances, you need to identify what went wrong as well so you don't do it again. Once you essentially call it out, it stops holding so much power. Once you can admit to yourself that you engaged in a particular behavior, it silences the opposition.

Maybe you bought an expensive car and put yourself in

debt to look cool to those around you. Well, it's time to realize that if you have to have a certain type of car for someone to like you, perhaps that person is not someone you want to be hanging around with. Driving a Bentley or a Honda has nothing to do with who you are; it's about what kind of vehicle you bought. The same goes for if you bought a massive house so that you could blend in with a certain type of crowd that you want to be like. Know that a house means nothing about who you are. It's just a big pile of wood, concrete, and shingles. It's not your whole life, nor does it illustrate who you are as a person.

I've said it once, and I'll say it again. There's no need to beat yourself up over past mistakes. What you have to do is simply *stop* making the choices that got you into your current predicament. Start spending more wisely. Stop wasting money and stop buying things you don't need.

Chapter 5
FAITHFUL WITH LITTLE, FAITHFUL WITH MUCH

As you read this chapter, you are possibly in one of two places. One, you are a devout religious believer and welcome any discussion on God, Jesus, or the Bible. Two, you wholeheartedly want nothing to do with it. Whether you are one of those or something else entirely, stay with me, please. Give me just a moment to explain a principle that no matter what your religious belief, you will learn to love and recognize in your journey to healthy finances.

I remember the first time I ever picked up a Bible. I was in my early 20s and was so intrigued with how Jesus taught and how he used parables (short stories) in nearly all his teachings. I remember one of the things he said that has stuck with me for many years since I read it the first time. In the book of Luke, Jesus notes, "If you are faithful in little things, you will be faithful in large ones. But if you are dishonest in little things, you won't be honest with greater responsibilities" (Luke 16:10 NLT). When I read that for the first time, it resonated deep within me. I thought that if I can just be faithful with the seemingly insignificant things that most people take for granted, that it would help me in every area of my life. These "seemingly insignificant things" could be saving money, not spending too much, always telling the truth, or keeping promises you make to yourself and to others. Here I am, many years later, and these words still impact me just as deeply today.

This verse can clearly be applied to finances and the principles of how you handle money. Actually, nearly a third of all the teachings Jesus gave had to do with money. Think about that! While I can't sit down and interview Jesus as to why he talked about finances so much, perhaps Jesus made the same observation that I've made regarding peoples' spending habits. Money is all around us, and we are all using it. So, we need to have conversations about it. We also need to realize that there are principles that apply to our financial lives, and we are only causing ourselves grief if we think we can avoid them.

Waste a Little, Waste a Lot

Listen, if you completely blow your salary of $40,000, it's looking pretty certain that you are also going to blow your salary if it gets to $4,000,000. Don't believe me? Think about people that achieved celebrity status and are now broke. Quite a few names come to mind. Out of respect, I won't mention any of them. At the height of their celebrity, they got a few million dollars and realized they had hit it big. But after buying a few luxury cars and a multi-million-dollar home or two, their frivolous spending in every area of their life left them with no money and nothing to show for it. Even all the extravagant items they bought had to be sold in order to pay their creditors. Frankly, these situations are sad to watch when you can foretell where these spending habits will lead. You may laugh and think, "Well, I can't afford luxury items, Ronnie, and I have never owned any." Yes, but is what you're buying over your limit? That's what you need to be cognizant of in all you do. The good news is that you need not fret if you haven't been faithful with the little you have. You can start today. Begin faithful practices in your finances, and you won't have to wait too terribly long to see results.

Margin

One financial principle that I rarely hear people talk about is *margin.* It's a powerful tool and a way of thinking that can revolutionize your finances. Margin is the distance between you and your limit in any area of your life. Here are some examples to help you see how it applies to our lives. If you have to be at work at 7:00 a.m., then 7:00 a.m. is the limit. If you arrive past that, well, bad things happen. So, of course, you know that you want to arrive before that time. The amount of time between when you arrive and when you are supposed to arrive is the margin in that area. So, in this example, if you arrive at work at 6:55 a.m., you have 5 minutes of margin. Similarly, if you have $150 to spend on groceries, $150 is the most you can spend. If you spend anything past that, you will be beyond your limit and you're going to have to put something back on the shelf. Obviously, you've given up spending on credit, *right*? So, if you spend $140 on those groceries you planned to spend $150 on, there's $10 of margin left in that transaction. Do you see how easy this is!

Margin is a great thing. Not only is it great, but it's absolutely necessary if you want to get to a place of financial health. It's a wonderful and fabulous part of how we can advance in life. But when it comes to finances, many people all over the globe have zero margin in their lives. They can't arrive early anywhere because they're too busy to allow extra room in their schedules. If they get a check for $500, that check is going right out the door. Most people, even if they have outstanding bills that $500 could help them make some headway on, spend that money on luxury items they don't need. It's as if money in the bank causes the desire for spending rather than the desire for saving. But guess what? You're reading this book now, and you're about to become a margin champion—and here's how you do it.

In every purchase you make, consider margin. You're walking down the aisle in your favorite grocery store and you pause between the chips and soda. On one side of you is your favorite kind of chips, and on the other side is your favorite soda. Each item costs $5. Now you *could* walk 10 more feet and go to the dreaded store brands, which would be a few dollars cheaper. I'm actually a huge fan of store brands just so you know. Now, you get to the store brands and see that you can get each item for $3 instead of $5. For all the math majors, you know that saves you $2 each and a total of $4 if you buy those two items. Choosing the cheaper brands creates margin in your total purchase. If your grocery limit was $100 total, you just created $4 more room by making a better and more economical choice.

As you continue to walk, your friend texts you and wants to hang out tonight. She wants to go for a nice dinner that will cost you $30. You want to see your friend, so you don't want to say you can't join her. You could text her back and suggest having coffee at a local shop. Instead of spending $30, you would then be making another good choice by getting an economical coffee that costs only $3 or so. In these two instances, you made good financial decisions that allowed more margin to come into your life. Over the long haul, you will find money is accumulating in ways you never thought possible.

The key is to be conscious that you need to accumulate margin. You should never cross the line by spending too much. But if you do, margin in other areas can cover you and avoid sending you farther into debt. But be aware that you need to know your limits in finances and never go beyond them. In doing so, always see how much margin you can put in between yourself and those limits. Squeeze every little bit of margin out of your life that you can. The more, the merrier.

You can even play a little game with accumulating margin. This is especially helpful if you are paying off debt or if you are out of debt and want to save money to invest. Every time you make a purchase, see where you can pinch a penny. Say to yourself, "If I get this item rather than that one, I can save $2 (for example). That's $2 I can use to get out of debt or that I can use to invest." It may seem like a minimal amount; but when you do it over and over, it accumulates into big savings. You should always be thinking about how you can save and how that money can go toward getting you out of your current position. Then you can get into a new position with more freedom to do what you want in life.

Grab your financial journal and jot down a few places where you need to build in some margin and write down some ways you can do so. Sometimes creating a little space in a few areas of your finances isn't too difficult. Also, the benefits you receive from creating that extra room will be more than worth it!

Dishonest?

Let's revisit the statement made by Jesus, which I quoted at the beginning of the chapter. He said, "If you are faithful in little things, you will be faithful in large ones. But if you are dishonest in little things, you won't be honest with greater responsibilities" (Luke 16:10 NLT). You may be reading that statement and wondering about the second half of it. You may be trying to figure out why on earth I threw a statement at you about being dishonest—whether it is in little amounts or large amounts. You may be thinking this doesn't apply to you because you haven't done anything dishonest in your personal finances. But listen, if you have put yourself into debt and spend more than you make, you have been dishonest with yourself!

You have spent money that you don't have and therefore have been dishonest with yourself about what you are able to spend. If you walk out of a store with clothes that you don't have money for, did you really buy them? If you drive a car that has a lien on it, the bank actually owns it; you just get to drive it and put it in your name. That's why if you don't make your payments, the bank sends the repo man to come and retrieve the car from your driveway. Buying on credit is certainly okay to do; but if you get yourself into serious debt trouble, you have been dishonest with yourself and that's not what any of us wants to do.

Too Much Too Fast
On the topic of dishonesty, consider this example. I have a pre-teen son. He's a great kid. He's smart, determined, and works hard at whatever he does. But let's say that I want him to have great things, and I start to give him things he may not be ready for. So, let say I go out and buy him a brand spanking new Porsche. I try to help him keep his attention on the road, so I get him an automatic; and I never want him to be late anywhere, so I buy the fastest one available. I come home, throw him the keys, and say, "Have at it!" You and I both know he's going to drive that car into a ditch or into the side of someone's house in the first 10 seconds! Why? Because he's not ready for it!

You, too, need to be ready to handle increases in your finances. You need to first implement the practices outlined in this book before you are able to handle having more money in your pocket. We all want a million dollars in our bank account. But we need to be ready for it. We need to be ready for an increase. And the best way to do that is to do just what Jesus said. We need to be cognizant of whether we are being faithful with little or whether we are being dishonest with little. Are we being honest with ourselves? When we begin to be up-front with ourselves, we open up the doors for an increase to come our way and for us to handle what we receive.

The Way the World Works

I just gave you the example of my son in a Porsche. And of course, we all know that any parents in their right mind wouldn't do what I described. When we talk about a principle of being faithful with little and being faithful with much, we may lose sight of what it even means to be faithful with something. C'mon, we see it all around us. Everyone wants things yesterday. Yet, this is not how life works. For the really good things, we have to wait.

Picture someone graduating from college. Let's call him John. When John graduates, he knows that he wants to be successful. The first thing he does is look through the job postings, and he finds that a large company in New York City that needs a high-level executive. The company has placed the job opening on an online job board like it does for all of its job openings. John is excited—so excited he fills out an application. Without thinking too much of it, he goes through all the qualifications and writes up a résumé that includes everything the company is looking for and sends it in. Not sure about you, but I can already feel anxiety for what is about to happen to this guy. Sure enough, because he sounds great on paper, the company reads the résumé and brings him in for an interview.

The second John walks into the interview room, the interview team seems confused, as his résumé is quite extensive and there is no way he could have all this experience and still look this young. Obviously, the gig is up, and John is quickly found out to be a fraud. But where exactly did the error occur here? No, really. Where did the error occur in this story? What exactly went wrong? Well, let me tell you my rendition of what I see going on in a story like this and what the true crime in all of it is.

When someone lies, it's obviously wrong. But that really isn't the crux of the issue here. The issue is that John thinks he is entitled to something that he hasn't worked for. Yep, that's the biggest problem here. And I would even go so far as to say that if you don't see it, you need to check the story again. A college grad makes up some stuff for a résumé—no big deal. As a matter of fact, people lie on résumés all the time; scary, I know! But the real issue isn't what he said on the résumé, but his thought pattern that led him to it. It's the *root* of what caused him to write untruths in the first place. You see, he wrote something on paper that wasn't true. But what precipitated that action? It was a belief. Let me say that again. It was a belief that caused him to write what he did on the résumé. He believed he should have the job that he really shouldn't have, so he lied and manipulated his way to what he thought would be an executive position. Just so you know, we do this with finances. We want an outcome that we haven't earned and shouldn't have, but we get it anyway with buying on credit. We do things we shouldn't do to get things we don't need, and it causes us untold grief in the long run.

Beliefs Dictate Actions

Beliefs. Like it or not, they dictate what we do. John believed that he was entitled to an executive position even though he was in no way qualified. His belief led him down a wayward road. It caused him to lie on a résumé to get a job he wanted. If he had believed, in fact, that he wasn't ready for that job, he would have taken different actions.

And truthfully, if you are graduating college and want to be a CEO, do what it takes to get there. What does that include? It takes hard, honest, dedicated, and focused work—without lying or other shortcuts. If a person believes that he or she is entitled to something without working for it, that person's beliefs will not dictate proper actions. And that is what I want to camp out on here: how your beliefs dictate your actions.

You Move Toward Your Beliefs
Imagine you are enjoying an amazing dinner in a 500-seat banquet hall. I am standing on a stage talking to everyone when I suddenly have a premonition that terrorists are about to come in the back door and shoot at everyone. I know, graphic, but stay with me. Now, what I also know in this premonition is that these terrorists are coming only into the back door, and none of them are entering by the front door. I know that if we would just stand up and calmly walk out of the venue, we would all survive. We could then call the authorities, and everything would be okay.

What would you do? Well, I'll tell you what you would do. If you believed me, you would stand up and get the heck out of that building! You would be happy to find out this information and gladly leave your food behind, knowing that you would live to see another day. Now, what if you didn't believe me? You would be sitting there wondering whether I had lost my mind or whether I needed to be drug tested or something for coming up with a story like that. Let's be honest: You would likely be at the table laughing at those who were leaving. Your beliefs would dictate your actions, and what you believed would greatly impact what you do.

Or, let's say you and I are on an airplane. Not just any airplane, but a private Learjet flying from New York to Los Angeles. We are on our way to a Hollywood party where you get to meet lots of movie stars. You're super excited; it's the trip of a lifetime. About halfway there, over the middle of nowhere, I say to you that the plane is going to run out of gas in 1 minute. There is no way to land the plane in that amount of time, and it is going to crash. To survive, we have to jump out of the plane. I hand you a parachute and tell you we have to jump in a matter of seconds to do it safely. As I'm talking, I open up a back hatch to jump out. Now I can tell you one thing. If you believe you are about to go down in that plane, you will have no issues whatsoever jumping. But if you thought I was crazy, you would quickly begin to talk me out of my position. Your beliefs will determine what you decide to do. If you don't think the plane is going down, you will not be too keen on strapping a parachute to your back and jumping out of the plane while it's hurling through the sky.

What should you take away from these stories? That what you believe will dictate your actions. And that principle absolutely, without a doubt, will apply to your finances. If you think, like John, that you are entitled to things you are not, it will show in your actions. If you *think* that you need a $50,000 car and you have only $500 to your name, it will show up in your purchases. And frankly, with thought processes like that, it will cause you to go into debt that can ravage your life. If you can begin to believe, not that you deserve or need a $50,000 car, but that you deserve and need to have financial security, you're on your way to great things. And know that if you start to believe that you deserve to have margin in your finances, that you deserve to have money in your savings account, and that you deserve to retire and have money later in life, *then* you will begin to act accordingly and bring about positive change in your life.

Change Your Beliefs, Change Your Actions

If you want to change an action in your life, you have to begin with your beliefs. If you don't think that eating fast food every meal of your life is unhealthy and it's what you want to eat each meal, you without a doubt will be headed toward a drive-through every single meal of the day. But here's where it gets interesting.

You see, we have gone over a lot of things concerning your finances and how to get them straight. But at this point, you need to change the way you think about money. If you truly believe that having a nest egg of savings is better than having brand new clothes each month, you are on your way to saving more. If you think it's better to live well below your means so that you have more money set aside to invest, you are starting to believe correctly. If you are thinking that you want to live even further below your means, so you have money to give regularly—to honor the principle of giving—then you are truly going in the right direction. If you can change your way of thinking, you can then slowly begin your journey toward financial health.

Take time now to write down in your financial journal some ways you can change your thinking with regard to your spending, debt position, and savings.

Chapter 6
SAVING AND INVESTING

Saving and investing are perhaps the simplest and easiest elements to do compared with the other areas of financial health discussed in this book. At the same time, these are things that few people do. Putting money away for retirement, investing for wealth, and learning how to make your money work for you is not rocket science. With that said, if you're looking for a book on how to go to Wall Street and make millions overnight, this book isn't it.

    I have met people who wero multi-millionaires, millionaires, and then those who had plenty, but hadn't quite made it to millionaire status yet. What is interesting is that I have yet to meet one person who made it to that status all in one day—not even close. Everyone I talk to in my personal life who has millions or close to a million dollars has taken years to get there. They have developed habits and principles of financial health, and over the years, these have paid off. Stop thinking of waking up one day to money falling out of the sky; it's not going to happen. Financial health takes hard work and patience, which together are going to propel you to where you need to be in your finances.

The thing that I most want to get across here is that you don't have to be a Wall Street genius to have your money work for you. Investing in retirement is not some daunting task that is going to take a college degree to even understand how to start. In the following pages, I describe how you need to see everything as an investment. Everything you put money toward is an investment in some way. You need to adopt this mindset and make it a lifestyle.

A Tale of Two Checks

There were once two men. Both of them worked for the same company, and both were very successful at what they did. Their boss decided to give them each bonus checks for $25,000. Each of them went home and told their spouse about the checks, and both families were very excited about the bonus and all that it was going to bring.

What is interesting about these families is that the two made very different decisions about what to do with the

$25,000. Here's how it went down. Once each person got home and discussed what to do with the money, both concluded that they should "invest" the money in something that would be worthwhile so they could get more out of it. Each family was ecstatic and made up a plan of what to do from there.

The first family was financially responsible and had been living below their means for some time. When they got the $25,000 check, they called an investor and said they wanted to invest in some quality mutual funds. They spoke over the phone for some time and, with the help of the professional, got a plan together for the investment. They were happy about what they were doing and felt it was a good thing to do with their $25,000.

The second family was living paycheck to paycheck. They didn't have any debt, but they were just right on the line each month of not having enough to pay for everything. They thought about the money, and while thinking decided they didn't want to drive their old car anymore. Nothing was wrong with it, but they wanted to invest the money in themselves. They wanted to do something that would make them happy, and they knew that a brand spanking new car would do the trick. They went out and paid cash for the car and, just like the first family, felt great about the investment they were making.

As time went on, the two checks that had obviously gone toward two different things began to go in different directions. The stock market as you know can fluctuate, but for the most part, produces a return over the long run if you invest intelligently. I'm not talking about day trading, nor am I talking about trading volatile stocks. I am talking about investing in quality funds with a good performance record. A vehicle or other things generally do the opposite; it goes down in value. Let's just say that the car went down in value 5% per year. It's usually more than that, but for the purposes of this story, let's figure 5% each year. At the end of just 5 years, the car that cost $25,000 would be worth $19,344.

Let's say the other family checked its investment account after 5 years as well. Now instead of losing 5% like the car did as it aged, the investment went up by the same amount of 5% as the mutual funds they had invested in began to grow and produce a return. And let me say, this is not an insanely high rate of return. This is an extremely possible rate if money is invested in quality funds selected with the help of a professional. The $25,000 investment the second family made had grown to $31,907 by the end of 5 years.

So, while both families started off with $25,000, in 5 years one had something worth $31,907 and the other had something worth $19,344. Which person would you rather be at the end of that 5 years? There was a $12,563 difference in what they had at the end of 5 years. And I'm not sure about you, but I would like to be the second family who had their investment go up.

The reason I am going over this is not to keep you from buying cars; you need them, and you're going to have to buy one sometimes—just be smart about your purchase. But my point has nothing to do with cars. What this illustration is about is to show you about how money works and how you can invest it into your future for a better life for you and your family. I am by no means an investment specialist. I always advise people to use the help of a professional when investing. I know, there are ways to do it yourself; but when it comes to investing, I don't mind paying someone to help me along. I am fully aware that some of the top professionals in the field have spent years researching different ways to invest. They have taken that time to hone their profession, and it's wise to seek their counsel when investing. What I want to communicate here is not how to invest, but how you need to change your mindset into an investment mindset. I don't mean that every dollar you get goes into the stock market, but that when you spend money, you see every purchase as an investment, and you consider what it's doing in the long run rather than a short term.

Retirement

Retirement. The word just sounds good. It usually is accompanied by thoughts of sitting on a beach, being out on a lake fishing in your boat, or just sitting on the porch thinking about what you are going to do today. But retirement looks different for a lot of people. One thing that it does look like for some is nonexistent. For some, there is no chance of retirement; instead they will be working until they die. This may or may not be what you want to do, but either way, if you prepare, you can have an income stream coming in and work only if you want to. If you don't have that stream of income, you won't have the luxury of deciding whether or not to work. You will for certain be working so you can eat and live.

One thing is for sure: If you don't begin saving for retirement, you will likely have to work until the day you die. I don't want this for you. Maybe you love your job and you are okay with doing it forever. In that case, I at least want you to have the option of taking a lot of time off when you are past retirement age. For those guys I talk to who are 25 and say that they don't care about retirement, I always tell them that they will when they are 65. We sometimes put off thinking about and taking action for our retirement;

but the earlier you start, the better off you will be.

You can make the decision to save and invest in your retirement now and live it up later, or you can live it up now and do without later. It's always best to pay the price now and enjoy the fruit later. This is long-term thinking at its best. If you can begin now to invest in your future, I can promise you that you will thank yourself at 55, 60, or 65, or whatever age you decide to retire and cash in on what you have invested in. I have been walking this earth for some time now, and I have yet to meet a person who regretted planning for retirement. But I have met, in large numbers, people who did absolutely nothing to plan for their retirement and have to work just to put food on the table. Usually, at that point, they are at an age where waking up and working is not what they are looking to do. With all that said, please be sure you take the time to prepare and invest for retirement.

But I Need My Money, Now!

I get it; you may not want to put a few hundred dollars into your account each month that you could be blowing on entertainment and needless spending. But haven't we gone over this already? It's things like that which keep us from retiring. Heck, the money most people spend on overpriced coffee on their ride to work could be put toward their retirement, and if accrued for enough time, would be a retirement with more than $1,000,000 savings.

Don't believe the last statement? Let me fill you in. If you spend $5 a day on coffee and buy it each working day, that is 20 coffees a month. It may be more, but I'll make it only 20 to prove my point that even less can make a difference. Those 20 coffees at $5 each cost you $100 a month. I'll do the math for you: $100 invested monthly for 40 years (between the ages of 25 and 65) with a 12% return rate would get you $1,030,970 for retirement. Yes, go ahead and peel your jaw off the floor! You need to be saving for retirement, and you need to be saving early. We discussed interest and how it works, and this example is a great one for you to see how time is your best friend in investing. That interest rate may seem high, and you may think it's not possible. But take time to do some research on the S&P 500 (many times considered the best gauge of the NYSE as a whole), and you will see this return rate is not impossible.

If you began investing $100 a month at the same return rate, but waited 10 more years until age 35, with only 30 years of investment, you would retire with only $324,351. Those additional 10 years of investing mean much greater returns in later years. This is because of how interest works. It's slow to begin, but once interest goes to work, the payoff gets higher and higher toward the end. But remember, investing can work for you or against you, so be sure that you are making it work for you!

401(k)s and IRAs

In the world of retirement, there are two extremely popular types of accounts you need to know about. The first is called a 401(k), and it is an employer-offered retirement program. It's called this because 401(k) is the actual section of the tax code it's in. These accounts are really good because they often come along with a matching percentage. A typical way this could work is your employer agrees to match your contributions up to a maximum of 3% of your total annual salary. If you make $50,000 a year, that 3% would be $1,500. So, this means when you put $1,500 into your 401(k), your employer would then give you an additional $1,500 to match your contribution. There are many different ways in which employers may do this, but most times these are great perks and you need to take advantage of them.

Also, because a 401(k) is done through your employer, it usually gives you access to an informed professional who can help you understand how it works. 401(k)s are highly favored as far as retirement options go because of the aforementioned matching contributions you can get from them. They vary depending on where you work, so check with your employer to find out whether there is a matching contribution and, if so, how much it is. If there is a matching option, I would suggest investing the maximum amount your employer is willing to match, or more. Another good thing is that your contributions are taken out before your pay is taxed, so it helps you out a bit there too. So overall, if you have access to a 401(k), my call is to always invest in it without a doubt.

An IRA is another type of retirement account, and it's defined as an Individual Retirement Account. This could be the route you would take if your employer did not offer any 401(k) benefits and you wanted to start a retirement account yourself. You can also have an IRA in addition to a 401(k). Why have two retirement accounts? Because you'll be reaping from two investment streams when you retire! If you go the route of getting an IRA, you need to sit down with someone who can personally talk over their advantages and disadvantages and how they would apply to you and your future plans. Some may favor one type of IRA over another, but it's going to be a decision you will have to make, and I recommend using professional help to make these important choices. You will be glad you did over the long haul.

Now, if you already have a 401(k) and/or IRA, you may

want to consider increasing your contribution each month. Now that you have seen examples of how interest works, you can see that a little investment now can be a huge return later and that, if you are living below your means, you won't miss that extra money you are contributing to your retirement. But you will, for sure, be thankful for it when you retire. You can increase the savings and investing percentage of your budget as you begin to make more gains in your financial practices. Once you are out of debt and have more money to allocate to savings, you can begin increasing the amount you spend toward saving for retirement and max out these investments. Again, you will do this if you are able to do so while staying within the percentage ranges set for your budget.

People to Help

One point I want to drive home is to make sure you have people to help you. You may have someone at your place of employment that can help, or you may need to call an investment professional. But I want to implore you not to delay in investing in your retirement. And whatever you do, do not completely forego investing for retirement all together just because you do not understand how it works. Not understanding investing has kept thousands of people from retiring in the fashion that they could have. I do not want you to be one of those people. There are resources galore on how to do this, and many of them are only a single phone call away.

Take the time to find people who can help you. Whether you can speak to someone in your office building or you call and go for professional advice, the point is to take action. There are experts in the field who can help you choose what is best for you. My wife works for an amazing company and, at any time, she can just pick up the phone and call someone to answer any questions she has concerning her retirement package. While everyone may not have that, many more do than you may think. Take the time to find out, if you haven't already, and immediately go to work at saving for your retirement if you have it available through your employer.

Long Term In or Long Term Out

There are two questions that I want you to train your mind to ask. As you get your finances together, first ask yourself, "Is this an investment?" Second, always ask yourself, "Is this investment long-term?" Believe it or not, nearly every financial decision you can think of can be filtered through these two questions. For example, you go grocery shopping and bring home food. You may be thinking that the food is eaten and there can be no investment there;

well, what about your health? You can invest in food at the grocery store that would diminish your health but give a quick shot of happiness as you gorge on pizza and ice cream. Or, you could have a spinach salad and invest in your long-term health. When you go to the gym, you could see it as money you spend so you could look cool in front of your friends; or you could see it as a time when you are investing in your health. See, everything can be an investment. When you build habits into your life in all types of areas, it will become easier for you to make the best choices with your finances.

As you look at where you spend your money, begin to think about the long-term return. You can consider your spending in terms of a single year, 5 years, 10 years — it's up to you. But what I can almost guarantee is that whatever time frame you use, you will see either an uptrend of an expense making a long-term gain in your life or a long-term loss. It's usually pretty clear to see which way it's going. Just like tho story of the two families that received $25,000 checks, they started off going in ono direction (with a gain or loss) and kept going in that direction for the long haul. You will see these things happening throughout your finances. *You just have to take the time to consider and begin to write in your financial journal what different areas you have in your finances and whether they are going in a positive or negative direction.*

Stocks

Stocks and the general idea of trading on Wall Street get a lot of people excited. I've known guys who watch a YouTube video or hear something from a friend about all the money to be made on Wall Street. They are all ready to get online, start an account, and become a trading maniac. Well, before you mount your horse and go traversing through the world of trading, I need you to listen to me. I am a fan of investing and very much like long-term options. But if you think you are going to go online and start making thousands of dollars a day in trading stock, you need to slow down a bit. At least at first.

Are there people out there who make lots of money in the stock market? Of course, there are! Are there day traders who make a living trading stocks day in and day out? For sure! But for every person who does that, there are at least nine who go broke. It's like a poker table. There is a guy who wins, but don't forget that he walks away with money that came out of the pockets of the people that he played against. If you are in financial trouble and trying to get your finances straight, I advise you to stick with slow, long-term investing for retirement at first. Then, if you want to build wealth, consider investing in a high-performing investment portfolio with the guidance of a professional financial advisor.

Please do not just hop on an Internet site and start trading because you heard your buddy say it was easy. Take your time and be patient. We are here to get your finances in order, not to make you a millionaire overnight. As a matter of fact, any time you see something that promises you to get rich quick, I implore you to get away from it. True wealth takes time. For now, let's get some good principles under your belt for now before we turn you into a trading genius.

A Penny a Day

We've talked about interest, but there's another financial principle you need to grasp. Consider this example. Let's say some guy walks up to you and makes you a proposition. He says he will give you $100,000 or a penny doubled every day for 30 days. When you hear $100,000, your jaw nearly hits the ground. The alternate offer is a measly penny doubled each day. How good could that be? Well, let's say you take the $100K because you believe that's a smart decision. But as you walk away, you ask the guy, "Hey, what would that penny doubled come out to?" You begin to smile as you think about how well you did until he tells you that on day 30, that penny would have been worth $5,368,709! "No way!" Well, it's true.

This is the great secret of compounding money. Think about it. A penny doubled each day would go 1 cent, 2 cents, 4 cents, 8 cents, 16 cents, 32 cents, and on day 7, it's at 64 cents. Get the picture? Well, a quarter of the way through, you will be at about $1. But on day 28, you cross the $1 million mark, and on day 30, that penny is worth more than $5 million. The doubling doesn't add up to much until the later part of the month when the amount starts to get big. And once you get down to the last few days, things get crazy.

Your savings and investments may not seem like much at first, but you need to stay in the boat for some time. And once you do, things can begin to show a greater return over time. You just can't jump ship too quickly. Realize that the type of compounding we're discussing works well for investing, but it can also work against you if it goes to your credit card company. Know how money works and use it to your advantage in every case you can.

Chapter 7
SOWING AND REAPING

So, you're out at your mailbox one day and you see your neighbor coming toward you. He looks upset as he nears you, so you start a conversation with him to see what is going on. He begins by telling you about his garden and how he's not having much success with what he planted. The two of you walk over to his backyard to check out his garden. You see a number of tomato plants, and they actually look to be doing okay. But your neighbor is furious as he plods around in the garden area. He says, "This is ridiculous! There isn't a single cucumber! No pumpkins! And I wanted peppers for my salads! There's not a single one here!"

You seem puzzled and again see only tomatoes. You ask him where he planted the cucumber, pumpkin, and pepper seeds so you can see what happened. His response is, "Well, I didn't plant those, I only planted tomatoes. But I really wanted some cucumbers, pumpkins, and peppers!" At this point, you would obviously think this neighbor has lost his mind. You would either laugh at him or get a bit terrified at his insanity and quickly walk back home. But, this type of thing happens every single day in people's financial lives. *People can see the principle of sowing seeds for vegetables, but when it comes to money, the principle is lost.*

Financial Seeds

Every single time you make a transaction, you sow a financial seed. If you buy Starbucks® every day, you are sowing toward your morning coffee. If you save 10% of your income, no matter how much you are making, you are sowing toward your savings. If you buy $1,000 worth of clothes each month at the mall, that is a seed that you are sowing. In all those examples, what you sow toward will grow. If you get a $5 coffee each morning instead of making a cup at the house, you are sowing a seed into a business's pocket. You get the enjoyment of the coffee's flavor, the caffeine, and the rush of going to one of those establishments. If you pay $1,000 for clothes each month, you are sowing toward fashion. You will have an amazing wardrobe and, depending on what you buy, you will look amazing wearing it!

But here's the kicker. What do you want in your garden? If you picked up this book, you are possibly in a bad financial situation. If you are, you need to sow toward being out of debt, having a savings account, and having margin in your spending. In that case, it's ludicrous to spend hundreds of dollars a month on clothes. It is also just as ludicrous to spend $5 on a coffee that you could make at home for a quarter. I know I keep bringing this up, but it's a major money waster I see going on time and time again.

Look, if you make $300,000 a year and are debt free, then go for it! But I talk to people time and time again who are up to their eyeballs in debt, live paycheck to paycheck, and haven't had any savings in decades. But guess what? They sow seeds toward everything else, except themselves. The won't sow to pay off the debt, they won't sow to save some money, but they will sow to high-end restaurants, toward a $35,000 car, a pair of $200 shoes, and $250 sunglasses. It makes my head spin. I sometimes ask people how on earth they think they are going to keep up these types of habits. They nearly always reply, "I don't know." Again, if you are doing this, don't feel bad, just take the action to stop the spending.

Begin to look at everything as a seed. Look at your

entire financial situation like a garden. What kind of plants do you see right now in that garden? Because whatever is growing there, I bet you want to see more savings. I bet you want to see less debt and more money in your pocket. This can't happen if frivolous and impulsive spending does not stop. Your transactions are seeds, and your financial life is your garden. Treat them both right.

Giving

When I bring up the topic of giving, some people give me grief and say, "Ronnie, I can't afford to give. I'm already backwards financially; I can't give stuff away." Well, I am telling you that if you are in financial trouble, you can't afford not to give. While I could certainly go a religious route on giving, I don't have to. Even atheists who have tons of money are, time and time again, known as huge givers. People who are not religious also talk about the importance of giving. Giving is a principle that is woven into the fabric of our beings and makes us who we are.

Don't believe me? Consider two bodies of water. One is a flourishing river, and one is a nasty swamp. What is the difference? One has water flowing through it, and the other has water coming in and never going out. For a body of water to be healthy and flourishing, it needs to have water moving through it—and your finances are the same. I don't mean that your finances need money flowing out into the hands of the local department store. I mean that you need to assign 10–15% of your income to go toward giving to others. Start with the minimum and see how that giving can change the world for the better. Not only is giving going to create a place for you to be a blessing to others, but it will allow you to have more joy in your life.

I personally always start with giving at least 10% to my local church. The other percentage you assign can then be allotted in ways that you feel are best for how you want to impact the world. But know that once you embrace the power of giving, you can then begin to truly feel the joy it is to help and love on others. *What better reason to have wealth than to be a blessing to others in the earth?*

What Do You Value?

What you spend your money on is a reflection of what you value. If you value having a really nice car, there will be one sitting in the driveway. If you value eating at nice restaurants, your bank statements will reflection those expenses. Jesus noted, "For where your treasure is, there your heart will be also" (Matthew 6:21 ESV). It strikes me that he says to *first* look to where your treasure is. Once you find that, you will see where your heart is. You can't tell me that you don't love buying new clothes when I can see from your bills the shopping you do each week. It's what you love. So, basically, determining what you value is an exercise to find what you love most.

You need to take time to look at your bank statements and your credit/debit card statements to see whether they really reflect where your heart is. If your money goes toward needless *stuff,* that really gets you nowhere. I like having cool stuff too, but in the end, it's not going to bring you true joy. I honestly think that wanting too much stuff means you over-value what others think; it means that you feel you need to get expensive items to look a certain way. But that isn't going to bring happiness. What is going to bring happiness is to align your wallet with what your heart truly values.

Want to Make More?

If you want to make more money, you don't necessarily need to start with figuring out what job or task will make the most money. Instead, I want you first to think about adding value to everything around you in your current position. What on earth does that mean? It means that you need to make it a point to make everything you touch better. It means that as you go about your work, you have a choice to do the bare minimum of what is asked, or you can do all you can to make every single situation you encounter better. This goes along with your tasks, your encounters with your boss and coworkers, and even the attitude you have while going about your day. By making everything you do better, you are adding value to it. If you are a teacher and are tasked with teaching a class you don't like, do all you can to make it the best class in the entire school and you will bring value to it. Don't like being a waiter or waitress? Do all you can to make the experience of those you serve the greatest restaurant experience they have ever had and thus bring value to the situation and to what you do.

Why on earth am I suggesting this? Because money is a natural consequence of adding value. If you add value to the marketplace, money is coming your way. If you are in a position you don't like and want to move up, excel above all those around you and add value to everything in your roach. There's a task no one wants to do? Take it on and knock it out of the park! This adds value to the you, your reputation, and the marketplace, and it's done by making everything that you touch better. This is one of those principles again that few embrace, but once you do, please know that you are on the way to the top.

How Businesses Really Make Money

Look at any successful business. What does it do that

attracts customers? What is the formula that brings people through its doors and gets them to hand over their cold hard cash? Well, it's that a successful business has created a product or service that adds value to people's lives in some way. People like to go to Walmart® and shop. It's one of the largest and most successful businesses in American history. It provides one-stop shopping with a huge selection of product choices and, as you know, offers them at a low price. Walmart adds value to the consumer by delivering a choice of low-cost and high-cost products, and so people continue to shop there.

Starbucks is another business that crushes a lot of the competition. You may be scratching your head thinking they only make coffee. But think about it, coffee is possibly the most divine thing on earth. And frankly, life does not begin until you have your morning cup of coffee. Okay, so you probably noticed how I feel about coffee; but think about it. Starbuck's not only delivers a high-quality product, but it also creates a brand and an atmosphere that people like. And guess what? If people like it, it adds value to their lives. For some people, the act of going to a Starbucks adds value to their day. You can think of it this way: People want to be happy. If you create a product or service that makes people happy, they will pay you to get it. It's because you are essentially delivering happiness to them.

It's the principle of adding value, and it works every time. Whether it's Starbucks, Walmart, or any other place where you like to shop, the successful business in some way adds value to your life and causes you to spend money there.

How You Can Add Value

I want you to get out your financial journal right now and start with a fresh page. Begin to brainstorm about how you can add value to the marketplace and to the world. Jot down anything that comes to mind. Maybe you have a million-dollar business idea or a way to give people joy, or both! You see, here's what's important, so please pay attention. Your idea has to be from the heart. It has to be something that is birthed from inside of you. Because when something comes from your own heart, it changes the product or service. When something comes from inside of you, you feel the need to make it happen, you feel the drive to move forward with it, and you foel why this product or service needs to be in the world.

When you not only see a problem in the world and maybe in yourself, and then you set out to fix it, *this* is where greatness comes from. It's the person who struggled with depression for years and overcame it that can help so many others who are struggling with it now. It's the person who has experienced bad coffee shops with no life in them that can come up with a new idea for how a coffee shop needs to look and feel. It's the mom who takes her child to daycare each morning who says to herself, "I know how this can be done better" that ends up revolutionizing the industry. It's all about what you feel in your heart and what you feel needs to be better in the world.

Anyone Can Change the World

I mean it when I say, "Anyone who makes the decision to do so can change the world." Anyone! But you have to make the decision to do so, and that decision has to begin with the idea of adding value to others. Right now, you may be putting together a plan in your financial journal for getting your finances together, and it is actually beginning to make sense to you. The piece you may be struggling with is how to move forward and make more money. I always caution people (and I'm doing it again): You need to get your spending under control and do that *first,* before you start increasing earnings. Don't start with how can I make more money? Start with how can I add more value to the marketplace? The money will follow.

If you are in a job that you don't like, let me speak to that for a moment. It happens all the time. You get a job because you need the money, and you secretly, or publicly, hate the job more than words can describe. I challenge you today to begin to work at that job not as an employee, but as if you were an owner. Why on earth would I tell you to do that? Because it will increase your joy! And in the end, you'll add more value to the marketplace as a happier employee. Your value goes up, and so will your pay eventually.

I don't care what you do for a living. You have to make the choice to say, "I am going to love what I do no matter what. I am going to make the best of every situation." And this is how you will begin not only to be happier in your job, but also to be more productive and feel better about what you are doing. And guess what? When you start doing better, you may get a promotion and start working your way up in the organization. Once you start feeling better, there's no end to how high you can go. Make the decision today to add value to whatever you do. Once you do that, search your heart for how you can add value to the world. Once you start taking off in that direction, your finances will begin to follow suit.

Chapter 8
THE POWER OF CONSISTENCY

Now that you've made great leaps and bounds toward getting everything in order with your finances, there's a little tool that you will need to keep going; that tool is consistency. If you've dug yourself out of a large amount of debt, there's a good chance that you have built new habits that benefit you in a big way. Maybe you've gotten into a habit of tracking your spending, maybe you've gotten into a habit of questioning every expense, or maybe you've made a habit of paying cash for everything. Whatever that habit is, you now need to keep going and be consistent. These are basic things, but if you can master them, they will forever alter the course of your life.

    Know from the get-go that it's going to be easy to get distracted. You may be tempted to take out a loan to build a $40,000 swimming pool in the backyard or to get a shiny new car like your neighbor down the street. If you get these impulses, remember where you came from. While taking a deep breath, slap your inner child a few times and remind it that debt was no fun and that you aren't going back there. Once you come to your senses, keep going down the path of freedom and think about how good it feels to actually have money in the bank.

Why the Gym Works for Some

I love the gym. It's a great place to go and lose some stress and feel good about yourself. What is interesting is a trend that goes on there that we are all familiar with. Each year January 1 rolls around and, with it, people resolve to get in shape. The New Year's resolution of losing weight and getting in shape is pretty much the biggest New Year's resolution around. The fact that Thanksgiving and Christmas come just before this critical time makes for a quality precursor.

January 1 is a time for all to say, "This year, I'm losing the weight and getting in shape!" But as the year rolls around, I can describe in detail the journey most will take without ever knowing them. They resolve to get in shape and lose the weight. They buy a gym membership, go to their local Target® and buy new gym clothes, and they decide to go to the gym 5 days a week. Then comes that fateful day. January 1 rolls around, and they're off! Never missing a gym appearance, eating every meal they planned to—it's a beautiful thing to see. But what ends up happening over time? Well, you can finish the story yourself, either because we all know what is going to happen, or maybe even you yourself do it each year.

Yes, most people who resolve to do better go to the gym less and less each week until they stop going, and they eat worse and worse food as the year goes on. Within a few months, most are right back where they were before they started. As a matter of fact, if you go to a gym of any kind, you can attest that in January, it is packed; and by the time February rolls around, attendance is back to normal.

What then is the magic pill—the anecdote that we all need? Well, while there is no pill, what we all need is a little thing called consistency. If we can be consistent, we can achieve what we want to. This goes for the gym goer and for the person who is getting their personal finances together.

Commitment

There's more to learn from some gym goers than just the fact that they are likely to fail. Have you ever wondered why? Think about it. They made a resolution to go against the grain. They decided to pay money for a gym membership, to take time out of their day, to eat food they like less, to lift things that are heavy, and to run till they breathe hard. Essentially, they committed themselves to difficulty, and it wasn't as much fun as they thought. Usually, these gym goers work their rear ends off to lose only a pound or two a month, and that doesn't sit well with them. I mean, of course, it took them years to get out of shape; it's only fitting they should have six-pack abs in a couple of days, right?

You need to recognize that everything good comes from some sort of commitment. Look at the Olympic athlete, the million-dollar investor, the teacher who educates our children, the doctor who takes care of us. At some point in each of their lives, they made a choice to be committed to something. What you have to do is realize that this money thing is going to take commitment over the course of many years, and you need to get this early on so there are no surprises. Good saving and investing for 2 years and then 1 year of frivolous spending will only send you back to the debt cycle you worked so hard to get out of. Stay with it and don't give up. Be committed!

Hard Work

What some commit themselves to in the gym is a long and hard road. It is day after day in the gym while eating fewer calories and, basically, it is lots of arduous work. In the end, many quit so that they can do what is easy. And that is what happens with our finances. For a moment we may lose the debt or begin to spend right; but unless we embrace this long and difficult process, we have the tendency to fall right back into the same problems.

You worked on your financial journal and are off on a beautiful path to where you need to be. But after some time, you may be tempted to fall off the wagon because you realize it's difficult. I beg you not to fall away. It's going to possibly take years to get to where you need to be, and that's okay. If it took you years to accumulate debt, then it may not all go away in 2 days. It's just like the abs; you can't eat ice cream for 25 years and then, after eating a salad for lunch for 1 week, expect to be chiseled. It takes time.

Realize something for me. Realize that consistency is going to be what gets you to where you need to go. Yes, a few good decisions can get you moving in the right direction. But it's going to be consistency that keeps you on the right path. It's going to be so tempting at times to fall back into bad habits. Think about the person on a diet. After a while, that rice cake doesn't taste as good as it did when starting out with all that energy on day one. That can sometimes send a person to the fridge for an eating contest with only one contestant. This type of slip-up in your finances can send your life into havoc. You can have great finances, but overall you have got to get consistent in what you do to keep things going in the right direction. Getting your finances in order will take the same tenacity; but know one thing: You have what it takes, and you can keep this up for the long haul.

You're Going to Want to Quit
There are going to be days (and hear me on this) that you look at your entertainment budget and realize you are completely out of money for the month. You're only halfway through the month, and your friends are calling you wanting to go see the new movie that just came out. Inevitably, you may say to yourself, "It's just this once; a few bucks won't hurt me." It's at that point you head off to the movies and spend money out of your savings. And guess what? You spent it, and not only did you survive, but there's a chance that it actually felt good. You had a great time and feel that the spending was worth it.

At that point, it's likely that this may happen again. You are walking through a mall and see a pair of shoes you love that you can't afford. You know there's possibly a credit card in your pocket. Well guess what is about to happen? You guessed it, you're about to fall right back in the middle of all those poor spending habits. I bring up the example of the diet because the habits that are exhibited are usually pretty similar. I am here to let you know what you are likely to do here. You need to anticipate this temptation at the onset rather than running into it unexpectedly months down the road. If you can see the possibilities early on, you can steer to where you need to be later on.

Eyes on the Prize

I have played sports most of my life. Now that I'm older, I help my son play various sports. One thing that always cracks me up is a statement that you hear so much it becomes mind-numbing. No matter whether you are trying to hit a baseball, catch a baseball, catch a football, or countless other activities in countless other sports, you will hear the phrase, "Keep your eye on the ball." It's comical because it gets said so many times on ball fields around the country that it should just be etched into the fencing. But why is it such an important thing to do? Because if you don't, you will fail.

Kids all over the world are missing the ball when they try to hit it and dropping the ball when they try to catch it. This is happening because they simply aren't focusing on the ball—or, for lack of a better term, they are not looking at it. The same goes for your finances. You have to be looking at what you want to hit. Maybe it's getting out of debt; maybe it's saving a certain amount of money. Whatever it is, you have to be constantly focused on that goal. If you look away, you will be just like the 10-year-old boy who strikes out every time he goes up to bat—just because he isn't looking at what he is trying to hit.

If we can keep our attention where it needs to be, this whole process of getting out of debt or saving money can be easier. All the distractions of life can be just like the kid going up to bat. His best friend is in the dugout, the girl he likes is watching from the stands, and the sun is in his eyes. There are a lot of things competing for his attention, and more times than he wants to admit, they win his attention when they should not. When you are up to bat, don't be distracted by something shiny in the stands. There's a time for all of that, and the time is not now when you are trying to get things right with your finances. Stay focused and don't be taken away in the moment.

I, for one, bring up all of these things that can take you off course because I've fallen victim to them, as have a lot of people that I know personally. Don't think that you're bad or that something is wrong with you if you are having difficulties with your finances. It's okay, and you are going to do well with this! But one thing you will always have to do is keep your eyes on the prize as you go forward. What does that mean? It means you have to keep your goal of being financially fit at the forefront of your thoughts. If you want to do well with money, you have to always keep your financial plan at the forefront of your mind. If it's something you think about only occasionally, you will lose. If your eyes aren't on the prize of being financially fit, they are on the stuff that you want to buy. And that lull of wanting more stuff can get you every single time.

Positive and Negative

Consistency is oddly enough what overjoys me and scares me at the same time. I have seen it work both for and against people in ways that are overwhelming. If I could get people to save a mere $5 a day, it would turn out to be $1,825 in only a year. While that may not seem like much, I have run into countless people who would give their pinky finger to have $1,825 in savings. But they don't. They are on the opposite end of the spectrum, with no money whatsoever, living paycheck to paychock, and enough debt to make anyone's head spin.

On the flip side of consistency, as you can see, if you waste $5 a day, in a year you have put yourself in the hole $1,825. But what I am seeing is that these numbers go into the negative in much larger quantities. Consistency has been working against you for some time and, like I said, it's a neutral monster. You can feed it something good or something bad. What I can guarantee you is that when time is added, it only makes things grow. It's your choice what you want to feed it. But I beg you, look at what you are being consistent with and work toward applying consistency in all good directions.

Things Always Grow

There's a secret I want to let you in on. It's interesting to see how it works and, again, it can work to your advantage or your disadvantage. The secret is that everything grows (okay, so maybe it's not really a secret). Look out into the natural world. Right now, I am looking at a tree in my yard that is leaning over the roof of my house. I have recently had the conversation about how I need to cut it down saying, "If I don't cut it now, it will just get bigger." Or, have you ever planted a vegetable garden? Did you notice how the tiniest seeds can turn into big plants that produce food that you can actually eat? Or maybe it's your grass. No matter how much you may not want it to, it just keeps growing until the time comes when it needs to be cut.

For good or for bad, things in the natural world continue to grow, whether you want them to or not. What is interesting to me is how once the growth gets going in one direction, it takes a lot of effort to get it to go the other.

Mending Your Money

Once that tree gets to be 40 feet tall, it takes a lot of effort to get it down. When it's small, I might be able to trim some branches. But when it's big, I have to pay a tree removal service thousands of dollars to take it down.

Wherever you are right now in your financial situation, know that things are going to grow in the wrong direction unless you do something to actively bring them back to where they need to be. Maybe you're upset that you have a financial 40-foot tree in your backyard that is going to take lots of effort to get rid of. Right now, it's okay, but you just have to stop neglecting it so that you can remove it from your life. Continuing to ignore it or, worse, continuing to feed it will only result in it getting bigger and toppling over onto something else in your life.

The good news here is that good things also grow. If you can get your financial life on the positive side of things, you will see that the positivity begins to grow as well. When you save money, it becomes a habit, and your money begins to grow. When you invest, that money grows and brings along more money. You're going to have growth, whether good or bad. It's up to you to make sure that you're growing good things that are going in a good direction. Take the time to work toward consistency in your spending to make sure it is taking you in the right direction. You and I both know you can keep doing well in this journey, so don't disappoint either of us!

Don't Stop Believing in Yourself

In 1981 the band Journey released its classic song called Don't Stop Believin'. As soon as you read that, you may have begun singing the song in your head. Well, guess what, I want you to keep singing it. I want you to keep singing it because as you go down this road of getting your finances healthy, I need you to not stop believing. I need you to believe that you can do this, that you can get out of debt, that you can save money, that you can have an amazing retirement, and that you can teach others to do the same.

So much of what we do in life is about faith. And if you can have faith, you can change your finances in ways that you never thought possible. If you believe in yourself, you can achieve all your financial goals. Always remember that I believe in you. We may or may not ever meet, but as you work on your financial goals and work toward where you want to be, know that I believe you can do it no matter what!

THANK YOU!

Thank you for reading *Mending Your Money!* If you enjoyed it, please consider leaving an honest review. You can also send me feedback and/or follow me on social media. I look forward to hearing about the impact this book had on you and how you applied it to your life!

Instagram: @theronniekinsey
Facebook: Ronnie Kinsey

Made in the USA
Columbia, SC
03 April 2019